Trump's Wars: The Future of Global Conflict in a Polarized World

Introduction

The presidency of Donald J. Trump was one of the most polarizing and consequential periods in modern U.S. history. His tenure reshaped global alliances, redefined America's role in international conflicts, and heightened global tensions in unprecedented ways. His foreign policy, often dubbed the Trump Doctrine, was driven by nationalism, unpredictability, and an "America First" agenda that challenged conventional diplomatic norms. This approach led to both strategic victories and deep geopolitical fractures, the consequences of which continue to shape the future of global conflicts.

The Trump Doctrine: A New Era of Global Conflict

Trump's foreign policy was marked by aggressive economic sanctions, the undermining of international institutions, and a transactional approach to diplomacy. Unlike his predecessors, who leaned heavily on multilateral agreements and coalition-building, Trump often preferred unilateral action, relying on personal relationships with world leaders rather than traditional diplomatic channels.

His approach to China, for instance, escalated into a full-fledged trade war that had significant repercussions on global markets. By imposing tariffs and severing economic ties, he fundamentally altered the balance of power between the two largest economies in the world. Similarly, his hardline stance on Iran—marked by the withdrawal from the Joint Comprehensive Plan of Action (JCPOA) and the assassination of Iranian General Qasem Soleimani—pushed the

Middle East closer to chaos, reigniting conflicts that had been carefully managed through diplomatic means.

While Trump's supporters argue that his tough stance on global adversaries made America stronger, his critics contend that his erratic decision-making and isolationist tendencies weakened U.S. influence and created new geopolitical vulnerabilities. His administration's handling of NATO, for example, sowed distrust among allies, while his unexpected engagements with North Korea's Kim Jong-un, though historic, failed to yield long-term security agreements.

The Shift from Diplomacy to Aggression

One of the most defining characteristics of Trump's foreign policy was the rejection of traditional diplomacy in favor of a more combative stance. He frequently clashed with long-standing allies, demanding increased military spending from NATO members and criticizing organizations such as the United Nations, the World Trade Organization, and the World Health Organization. His administration viewed these institutions as ineffective and burdensome to American interests, a departure from decades of bipartisan support for global cooperation.

This aggressive posture extended beyond verbal rhetoric. Under Trump, the U.S. withdrew from the Paris Climate Accord, abandoned key arms control agreements, and redefined the role of the military-industrial complex. The increased use of economic sanctions as a weapon—especially against adversaries like Russia, Venezuela, and North Korea—exacerbated tensions rather than resolving them. While sanctions are often employed as a tool to force policy change, Trump's unilateral enforcement led to retaliatory measures that fueled further global instability.

How Polarization Shapes the Battlefield

Beyond military and economic confrontations, Trump's leadership deepened ideological polarization, both domestically and internationally. His presidency emboldened nationalist movements around the world, influencing leaders such as Jair Bolsonaro in Brazil, Viktor Orbán in Hungary, and Narendra Modi in India. This ideological shift toward nationalism and protectionism has created a fragmented global landscape where cooperation is increasingly rare, and conflicts are more likely to escalate.

At the same time, Trump's domestic policies—particularly his handling of racial tensions, immigration, and the media—had ripple effects on America's standing in the world. The erosion of democratic norms within the U.S. weakened its ability to advocate for democracy abroad, giving authoritarian regimes greater leverage. Countries such as China and Russia used America's domestic struggles as a propaganda tool, diminishing the U.S.'s moral authority on human rights and governance.

As the world moves forward, the consequences of Trump's wars—both literal and figurative—will continue to shape the global order. The rise of cyber warfare, economic realignments, and ideological conflicts are all part of the new battlefield that emerged under his administration. Whether the next leaders choose to reverse course or double down on Trump's strategies remains to be seen, but one thing is certain: the future of global conflict will be defined by the choices made during and after the Trump era.

This book will explore the wars that Trump waged—economic, military, ideological, and digital—and examine their lasting impact on the world. By analyzing the Trump Doctrine and its consequences, we will gain a clearer understanding of how global power dynamics have shifted and what the future holds for international relations in an increasingly polarized world.

Chapter 1
The Global Power Struggle Under Trump

The presidency of Donald Trump marked a significant shift in global power dynamics, challenging the traditional role of the United States as a stabilizing force in international relations. Unlike his predecessors, who largely upheld America's leadership in global institutions and alliances, Trump took a more combative and transactional approach to foreign policy. His "America First" doctrine prioritized national interests over multilateral cooperation, leading to strained alliances and new geopolitical rivalries. By questioning the relevance of NATO, imposing tariffs on both allies and adversaries, and pulling out of key international agreements, Trump redefined America's engagement with the world, creating a landscape of heightened uncertainty and competition.

At the heart of this global power struggle was Trump's aggressive stance toward rising powers, particularly China and Russia. His administration engaged in a heated trade war with Beijing, imposing tariffs and restrictions that escalated economic tensions between the world's two largest economies. Meanwhile, his relationship with Russia was marked by contradictions—while he expressed admiration for Vladimir Putin, his administration also imposed sanctions on Moscow, deepening hostilities. These conflicts extended beyond economic warfare to military posturing, cyberattacks, and ideological battles, making it clear that the global order was shifting toward a multipolar world where U.S. dominance was no longer unquestioned.

As the world adjusted to Trump's unpredictable foreign policy, other nations sought to fill the vacuum left by American disengagement. The European Union attempted to assert itself as a stronger independent force, China expanded its influence through its Belt and Road Initiative, and regional powers like Turkey, India, and Brazil took advantage of the shifting dynamics to pursue their own interests. The erosion of long-standing alliances and the rise of nationalist movements further complicated the global power balance, raising questions about the future of international cooperation and conflict. This chapter explores how Trump's leadership reshaped global power structures, setting the stage for a new era of international relations marked by uncertainty, competition, and shifting alliances.

Rewriting the Rules of International Alliances

Donald Trump's presidency disrupted long-standing international alliances, fundamentally altering the way the United States engaged with the world. While past U.S. presidents upheld global partnerships as pillars of stability, Trump viewed them through a transactional lens, demanding more from allies while threatening to withdraw from historic agreements. His "America First" doctrine led to a sharp departure from traditional diplomacy, fostering tensions with allied nations and reshaping the global balance of power. Under his leadership, institutions such as NATO, the United Nations, and the European Union faced unprecedented challenges, as Trump questioned their effectiveness and legitimacy. This shift had profound implications for the future of global cooperation, leaving behind an international landscape riddled with uncertainty.

One of the most significant ways Trump rewrote the rules of international alliances was through his stance on NATO. For decades, NATO had served as the backbone of Western security, deterring Russian aggression and maintaining transatlantic stability. However, Trump repeatedly criticized NATO members for not contributing enough to defense spending, accusing European allies of free-riding on American military power. He publicly called NATO "obsolete" and even threatened to withdraw the U.S. from the alliance if other member states did not increase their military expenditures. While his rhetoric led to some European nations boosting their defense budgets, it also weakened trust in the United States as a reliable security partner. Allies who had depended on American military support began exploring alternative strategies, with some European leaders discussing the creation of a more autonomous defense force independent of U.S. influence.

Trump's approach to alliances extended beyond NATO, as he also sought to renegotiate or withdraw from other key international agreements. He pulled the United States out of the Iran Nuclear Deal (JCPOA), which had been a multilateral agreement designed to limit Iran's nuclear capabilities in exchange for sanctions relief. His administration argued that the deal was flawed and did not adequately address Iran's regional aggression. However, by abandoning the agreement without securing a viable alternative, Trump not only escalated tensions with Iran but also alienated European allies who had invested in upholding the deal. Similarly, his decision to withdraw from the Paris Climate Accord signaled a retreat from global environmental cooperation, further isolating the U.S. from traditional allies who prioritized climate action.

Another key example of Trump's redefinition of alliances was his handling of U.S. relations with Asian partners. He engaged in a trade war with China, imposing heavy tariffs and sanctions on Chinese companies, which strained economic relations between the two superpowers. At the same time, he pulled the U.S. out of the Trans-Pacific Partnership (TPP), a trade deal designed to counterbalance China's growing influence in the Asia-Pacific region. This move left America's allies in Asia scrambling to maintain economic stability while allowing China to expand its regional dominance. Meanwhile, Trump's unpredictable relationship with North Korea, marked by both threats of military action and historic face-to-face summits with Kim Jong-un, left South Korea and Japan uncertain about America's long-term commitment to their security.

By reshaping global alliances through a mix of economic pressure, military threats, and diplomatic disengagement, Trump left behind a transformed international order. Some of his policies forced allies to become more self-reliant, while others created power vacuums that adversaries were quick to fill. As the world continues to adjust to the legacy of Trump's foreign policy, the future of global cooperation remains uncertain. Whether subsequent U.S. leaders will restore traditional alliances or continue Trump's disruptive approach will determine the long-term stability of the international system.

The Decline of Multilateralism

The presidency of Donald Trump marked a significant shift away from multilateralism, the principle that international cooperation and collective decision-making are essential for global stability. For decades, the United States had been a driving force behind multilateral institutions such as the United Nations, NATO, the World Trade Organization (WTO), and international treaties that promoted global peace, trade, and environmental protection. However, Trump's "America First" doctrine rejected the idea of shared global responsibility, favoring bilateral deals and unilateral actions over multilateral agreements. This shift fundamentally altered the global order, weakening long-standing alliances and creating a more fragmented international system.

One of the most striking examples of Trump's retreat from multilateralism was his withdrawal from key international agreements. In 2017, he pulled the U.S. out of the Paris Climate Accord, arguing that the agreement was unfair to American businesses and workers. This decision was met with widespread criticism from global leaders, as the U.S. had played a crucial role in negotiating the accord under the Obama administration. Similarly, Trump abandoned the Joint Comprehensive Plan of Action (JCPOA), commonly known as the Iran Nuclear Deal, despite opposition from European allies who had worked to keep the agreement intact. By exiting these agreements, Trump signaled that the U.S. was no longer interested in collaborative problem-solving, instead prioritizing short-term national interests over long-term global stability.

Trump's administration also undermined multilateral institutions by actively challenging their legitimacy and effectiveness. He frequently criticized the United Nations, calling it "just a club for people to get together, talk, and have a good time." His administration slashed U.S. funding for various UN programs, including the World Health Organization (WHO), which he accused of being biased toward China during the COVID-19 pandemic. The decision to withdraw from the WHO in the midst of a global health crisis was widely seen as a move that weakened global efforts to combat the pandemic. Additionally, Trump threatened to pull out of the World Trade Organization (WTO), arguing that it was unfair to

U.S. interests. His administration blocked the appointment of new judges to the WTO's appellate body, effectively crippling its ability to resolve trade disputes.

Beyond international agreements and institutions, Trump's rejection of multilateralism also had significant implications for global security. His frequent criticisms of NATO and his insistence that member nations increase their defense spending created tension within the alliance. While some countries did increase their contributions, Trump's rhetoric raised concerns about the U.S.'s long-term commitment to collective defense. Meanwhile, his preference for direct negotiations with world leaders—such as his controversial summits with North Korea's Kim Jong-un—often bypassed traditional diplomatic channels, making foreign policy more unpredictable.

The decline of multilateralism under Trump had long-term consequences for the international order. With the U.S. stepping back from its role as a global leader in diplomacy and cooperation, other nations—particularly China and Russia—sought to fill the void, expanding their influence in global institutions. The weakening of multilateral frameworks made it more difficult for nations to coordinate responses to global challenges such as climate change, economic instability, and pandemics. Whether future administrations will seek to restore America's commitment to multilateralism or continue Trump's more isolationist approach remains a critical question for the future of global governance.

America First: Consequences for Global Stability

Donald Trump's America First doctrine was a radical departure from the traditional U.S. approach to global affairs. Rooted in nationalism and economic protectionism, this policy prioritized

American sovereignty over international cooperation, reshaping how the United States interacted with allies and adversaries alike. While Trump and his supporters viewed America First as a necessary corrective to decades of global entanglements that they believed weakened U.S. economic and military power, critics argued that it eroded global stability, undermined alliances, and emboldened adversaries. By focusing on unilateral actions and rejecting multilateral diplomacy, Trump's policies triggered a chain reaction that reshaped international relations in ways that continue to have lasting consequences.

One of the immediate effects of the America First doctrine was the weakening of key global institutions. Trump frequently criticized international organizations such as the United Nations, NATO, the World Trade Organization (WTO), and the World Health Organization (WHO), arguing that they either took advantage of U.S. contributions or failed to serve American interests. He withdrew the U.S. from several major agreements, including the Paris Climate Accord and the Iran Nuclear Deal (JCPOA), despite opposition from European allies who had invested significant diplomatic efforts in maintaining them. His administration also threatened to withdraw from the WTO, claiming that it treated the U.S. unfairly in trade disputes. By sidelining these institutions, Trump's policies contributed to a decline in global trust in American leadership, leading some nations to explore alternative alliances and partnerships.

Another major consequence of America First was the escalation of economic conflicts, most notably the trade war with China. In an effort to reduce trade deficits and protect American industries, Trump imposed tariffs on billions of dollars' worth of Chinese goods, prompting retaliatory tariffs from Beijing. While these measures were aimed at reducing China's economic influence and reviving U.S. manufacturing, they had widespread consequences for global markets. The uncertainty created by the trade war disrupted supply chains, raised costs for American consumers and businesses, and slowed economic growth in multiple countries. Additionally, Trump's tariff policies affected not just China but also traditional allies such as Canada, Mexico, and the European Union, as he imposed tariffs on steel and aluminum imports, straining relations with long-standing economic partners.

Beyond trade and diplomacy, the America First policy had significant implications for global security. Trump's skepticism toward NATO and his insistence that European allies contribute more to defense spending created divisions within the alliance. While his pressure did lead to increased financial commitments from some member states, his repeated threats to withdraw from NATO raised concerns about the U.S.'s commitment to collective security. This uncertainty emboldened adversaries such as Russia, which expanded its geopolitical influence through cyber warfare, military interventions, and political destabilization efforts. Similarly, Trump's inconsistent stance on military engagements—such as his abrupt decision to withdraw U.S. troops from northern Syria, abandoning Kurdish allies—sent mixed signals about America's reliability as a security partner.

The broader impact of America First was a shift toward a more fragmented and unpredictable global order. With the U.S. retreating from its traditional role as a stabilizing force, power vacuums emerged that were quickly filled by China, Russia, and regional powers like Turkey and Iran. The erosion of multilateral cooperation made it harder for nations to coordinate responses to global challenges, from climate change to pandemic preparedness. While

Trump's approach did achieve some short-term victories, such as renegotiating trade agreements like the USMCA (United States-Mexico-Canada Agreement), the long-term consequences of America First raised serious questions about the future of global stability and America's role in the world. Whether future administrations choose to restore traditional alliances or continue Trump's unilateralist approach will shape the trajectory of international relations for years to come.

Chapter 2
U.S.-China Relations: A Cold War Reimagined

The relationship between the United States and China has long been complex, shaped by economic interdependence, military rivalry, and ideological differences. Under Donald Trump's presidency, tensions between the two superpowers escalated to levels not seen since the original Cold War between the U.S. and the Soviet Union. Trump's aggressive stance toward China—centered on trade, technology, and geopolitical influence—transformed the dynamic from cautious engagement to open confrontation. His administration imposed tariffs, restricted Chinese companies like Huawei, and challenged China's territorial claims in the South China Sea, fueling an environment of distrust. While the U.S.-China conflict had been brewing for years, Trump's policies accelerated a shift from economic competition to a broader struggle for global dominance.

The trade war became the most visible battleground in this new Cold War, with both countries imposing heavy tariffs on each other's goods. Trump justified these measures by arguing that China had engaged in unfair trade practices, including intellectual property theft and currency manipulation. His administration sought to pressure China into making concessions, but the retaliatory tariffs from Beijing hurt American farmers, businesses, and consumers. Beyond trade, Trump took direct aim at China's technological ambitions, banning Chinese firms from accessing critical American technology and urging allies to exclude Huawei from their 5G infrastructure. This technological decoupling signaled a deeper shift in U.S.-China relations, as both countries began to view each other as strategic adversaries rather than economic partners.

Beyond the economic front, Trump's policies also intensified military tensions in the Indo-Pacific region. His administration strengthened ties with Taiwan, increased naval patrols in the South China Sea, and expanded military cooperation with regional allies like Japan, India, and Australia. China responded with aggressive military maneuvers, heightening fears of direct confrontation. Meanwhile, ideological differences—such as Trump's harsh rhetoric on China's handling of the COVID-19 pandemic and human rights abuses in Hong Kong and Xinjiang—deepened the divide between Washington and Beijing. As a result, U.S.-China relations under Trump entered a period of sustained hostility, reshaping global geopolitics and laying the groundwork for a prolonged struggle between two competing visions of the world order.

Trade Wars and Economic Warfare

The U.S.-China trade war was one of the defining conflicts of Donald Trump's presidency, marking a dramatic shift from decades of economic cooperation to an era of heightened confrontation. As part of his America First agenda, Trump sought to reduce the U.S. trade deficit with China, curb what he saw as unfair trade practices, and limit China's growing technological dominance. His administration imposed aggressive tariffs on Chinese goods, restricted key Chinese technology firms, and pressured American allies to follow suit. In response, China retaliated with its own tariffs and economic measures, escalating tensions between the world's two largest economies. This trade war not only disrupted global supply chains but also signaled a broader shift toward economic warfare as a key tool of international rivalry.

At the core of Trump's trade war was his belief that China had long exploited the global trade system to its advantage. His administration accused China of intellectual property theft, forced technology transfers, and unfair subsidies to Chinese companies, creating an uneven playing field for American businesses. In 2018, Trump initiated a series of tariffs on Chinese imports, starting with $34 billion worth of goods and eventually expanding to over $360 billion. These tariffs targeted a wide range of products, from steel and aluminum to consumer electronics and agricultural goods. The goal was to pressure Beijing into making trade concessions, but the tariffs also had significant economic consequences for American businesses and consumers, leading to higher prices and supply chain disruptions.

China responded with its own countermeasures, imposing tariffs on U.S. goods such as soybeans, automobiles, and electronics, directly impacting American farmers and manufacturers. As the trade war intensified, both economies suffered. American companies that relied on Chinese imports faced increased costs, while Chinese firms saw declining exports to the U.S. The uncertainty created by the trade war led to market volatility, affecting investor confidence and slowing global economic growth. Despite efforts to negotiate, including the signing of the "Phase One" trade deal in early 2020, the core issues between the two nations remained unresolved. China continued to push forward with its industrial policies, while the U.S. maintained its stance on tariffs and restrictions.

Beyond traditional trade disputes, economic warfare extended to the technology sector, where the Trump administration took direct aim at Chinese tech giants. Companies like Huawei and ZTE were blacklisted, preventing them from accessing American semiconductor technology. The administration also pressured allies to ban Huawei from developing their 5G infrastructure, citing national security concerns. In response, China accelerated efforts to develop its own semiconductor industry and reduce dependence on American technology. This technological decoupling marked a significant shift in global supply chains, with both nations seeking to gain an edge in critical industries such as artificial intelligence, quantum computing, and telecommunications.

The U.S.-China trade war not only reshaped economic relations between the two countries but also had far-reaching implications for the global economy. As both nations hardened their economic policies, businesses around the world were forced to adapt to an increasingly fragmented trade environment. The era of open globalization began to give way to a new reality of economic nationalism and strategic decoupling, setting the stage for continued economic warfare in the years to come.

The South China Sea and Military Posturing

The South China Sea has long been one of the most contested regions in the world, with multiple countries claiming territorial rights over its vast waters, islands, and rich natural resources. However, under the Trump administration, tensions in the region escalated dramatically as the United States adopted a more aggressive stance against China's military expansion. The strategic importance of the South China Sea—both as a vital global trade route and as a region rich in oil, gas, and fisheries—made it a key battleground in the broader U.S.-China rivalry. Trump's policies reinforced America's military presence in the region while openly challenging Beijing's territorial claims, further straining diplomatic relations between the two superpowers.

China has long pursued an assertive strategy in the South China Sea, constructing artificial islands and militarizing key locations to strengthen its territorial control. The Chinese government claims nearly 90% of the South China Sea under the controversial "Nine-Dash Line," despite opposition from neighboring countries such as the Philippines, Vietnam, Malaysia, and Indonesia. Beijing has built military bases, airstrips, and missile systems on disputed islands, turning them into forward-operating military outposts. These actions have alarmed the international community, particularly the United States, which views China's territorial expansion as a direct threat to regional stability and freedom of navigation.

Under Trump, the U.S. responded with an increase in Freedom of Navigation Operations (FONOPs), a series of naval maneuvers designed to challenge China's territorial claims. American warships regularly sailed through the contested waters, directly passing near Chinese-claimed islands and asserting the principle that international waters should remain open to all nations. The U.S. also strengthened military alliances with regional powers such as Japan, Australia, and India through initiatives like the Quadrilateral Security Dialogue (Quad), reinforcing a collective response to China's military expansion. Trump's administration further escalated tensions by conducting high-profile naval drills, deploying aircraft carriers, and sending strategic bombers over the region, signaling a clear warning to Beijing.

China, in turn, responded with its own military posturing, conducting extensive military drills and increasing patrols by its navy and coast guard. The Chinese government repeatedly warned the

U.S. against "provocations," accusing Washington of destabilizing the region. Beijing's military also developed anti-access/area denial (A2/AD) capabilities, deploying advanced missile systems designed to keep U.S. forces at bay. In several instances, Chinese naval vessels engaged in dangerous maneuvers to intimidate American warships, raising concerns about a possible direct military clash.

Beyond military maneuvers, Trump's administration also took diplomatic actions to counter China's territorial ambitions. In 2020, the U.S. officially rejected China's claims over the South China Sea, aligning itself with the 2016 ruling of the Permanent Court of Arbitration in The Hague, which had deemed China's territorial claims illegal under international law. This marked a significant policy shift, as previous U.S. administrations had avoided directly taking sides in the territorial disputes. The Trump administration also provided military aid to regional allies like the Philippines and Vietnam, further complicating China's strategic calculations.

The growing militarization of the South China Sea during Trump's presidency underscored the increasing likelihood of conflict between the U.S. and China. While no direct military confrontation occurred, the aggressive posturing from both sides heightened the risk of miscalculation. As China continues to expand its influence in the region and the U.S. remains committed to countering Beijing's ambitions, the South China Sea remains a flashpoint that could shape the future of global security and U.S.-China relations for years to come.

Taiwan: The Next Global Flashpoint

Taiwan has long been one of the most sensitive and dangerous geopolitical issues in U.S.-China relations, and under Donald Trump's presidency, tensions surrounding the island escalated to levels not seen in decades. While the United States has maintained a policy of strategic ambiguity toward Taiwan, balancing its support for the island while avoiding direct provocation of Beijing, Trump's administration took a more confrontational approach. By strengthening diplomatic ties with Taipei, increasing arms sales, and openly challenging Beijing's claims over Taiwan, Trump fueled an already volatile situation. As China continues to view Taiwan as a breakaway province that must be reunified—by force if necessary—the island has become a potential flashpoint for a future global conflict.

One of the most significant policy shifts under Trump was the strengthening of U.S.-Taiwan relations. While previous administrations had cautiously supported Taiwan under the framework of the One China Policy, Trump pushed the boundaries by approving major arms sales to Taipei, including advanced missile systems, fighter jets, and naval equipment. The U.S. also increased its military presence in the region, with American warships conducting regular transits through the Taiwan Strait—a move seen as a direct challenge to Beijing. Additionally, high-level diplomatic engagements between U.S. and Taiwanese officials took place, breaking previous taboos that had kept such interactions limited. In 2020, then-Health Secretary Alex Azar became the highest-ranking U.S. official to visit Taiwan in decades, signaling a shift in Washington's willingness to publicly support the island.

China, viewing Taiwan as a core national interest, responded with increasing aggression. Beijing ramped up military drills near Taiwan, frequently sending fighter jets and bombers into Taiwan's Air Defense Identification Zone (ADIZ). The Chinese military also conducted live-fire exercises and amphibious assault drills, showcasing its ability to launch a full-scale invasion if necessary. The

People's Liberation Army (PLA) developed strategies to cut off Taiwan from potential U.S. intervention, including deploying advanced missile systems and bolstering its naval capabilities. Chinese officials repeatedly warned that Taiwan's increasing alignment with the U.S. was pushing the region toward war, and that any attempt by Taipei to declare formal independence would result in immediate military action.

The Trump administration's hardline stance on Taiwan had far-reaching consequences beyond U.S.-China relations. Regional allies such as Japan and Australia grew increasingly concerned about the potential for conflict, as any military clash over Taiwan would inevitably involve the broader Indo-Pacific region. The U.S. also strengthened military coordination with regional partners, reinforcing the Quadrilateral Security Dialogue (Quad) alongside Japan, India, and Australia to counterbalance China's growing assertiveness. Additionally, Taiwan itself responded to Beijing's threats by ramping up its defense capabilities, increasing military drills, and investing in asymmetric warfare strategies to deter a possible Chinese invasion.

Taiwan remains one of the most dangerous flashpoints in global geopolitics. The increasing militarization of the Taiwan Strait, coupled with the U.S.'s deepening support for Taipei, has made the prospect of a future confrontation more likely. While Trump's policies reinforced Taiwan's security, they also pushed U.S.-China relations to the brink, creating a legacy of heightened tensions that continues to shape global stability. Whether future U.S. administrations choose to maintain Trump's confrontational stance or seek a more diplomatic approach will determine whether Taiwan remains a peaceful partner or the center of the next great conflict.

Chapter 3
The Russia Factor: Friend or Foe?

The relationship between the United States and Russia under Donald Trump was one of the most controversial and ambiguous aspects of his presidency. Unlike previous administrations that treated Russia as a clear geopolitical adversary, Trump's approach was marked by a mix of diplomatic overtures, personal admiration for Vladimir Putin, and inconsistent policy decisions. While he publicly praised Putin and expressed a desire for closer ties, his administration simultaneously imposed sanctions on Russia, expelled diplomats, and took steps to counter Russian influence in various regions. This dual approach led to confusion both at home and abroad, raising questions about whether Trump saw Russia as a strategic partner or a persistent threat to U.S. national security.

Despite Trump's efforts to foster better relations, U.S.-Russia tensions remained high, particularly due to allegations of Russian interference in the 2016 U.S. presidential election. Intelligence agencies and congressional investigations concluded that Russia engaged in cyber operations and disinformation campaigns to influence the election outcome. These findings led to increased scrutiny of Trump's relationship with Putin, with critics accusing him of being overly deferential to the Russian leader. At the same time, Trump's administration took a hardline stance on some issues, such as increasing military aid to Ukraine, imposing sanctions on Russian officials and businesses, and expelling Russian diplomats in response to incidents like the poisoning of opposition figures. These conflicting signals created uncertainty about the true nature of U.S.-Russia relations during Trump's tenure.

Beyond election interference, Russia continued to challenge U.S. influence on the global stage, particularly in regions like Eastern Europe, the Middle East, and Latin America. Putin's government pursued aggressive policies in Ukraine, Syria, and Venezuela, often acting in direct opposition to American interests. In response, the Trump administration bolstered NATO's presence in Eastern Europe and authorized military support to countries threatened by Russian expansionism. However, Trump's frequent criticism of NATO and reluctance to confront Putin directly raised doubts about America's commitment to countering Russian aggression. As a result, the question of whether Russia was a friend or foe remained unresolved, leaving behind a complex and often contradictory legacy in U.S.-Russia relations.

The Trump-Putin Dynamic: Cooperation or Coercion?

The relationship between Donald Trump and Vladimir Putin was one of the most scrutinized and controversial aspects of Trump's presidency. Unlike previous U.S. leaders who treated Russia as a strategic adversary, Trump often expressed admiration for Putin, leading to speculation about the true nature of their dynamic. While Trump's rhetoric suggested a willingness to cooperate with Russia, his administration simultaneously imposed sanctions and took actions that countered Russian interests. This duality created an ambiguous relationship that left both allies and adversaries uncertain about the United States' position on Russia. The Trump-Putin dynamic fluctuated between moments of diplomatic engagement and geopolitical confrontation, raising the question of whether their interactions were based on genuine cooperation or underlying coercion.

Trump's approach to Russia was marked by an unprecedented level of personal diplomacy. He frequently praised Putin's leadership style, calling him a strong and respected leader, and dismissed concerns about Russia's authoritarian policies. Trump's skepticism toward U.S. intelligence agencies regarding Russian election interference in 2016 further fueled speculation about his motivations. The infamous Helsinki summit in 2018 became a defining moment of his presidency, where Trump, standing beside Putin, publicly contradicted U.S. intelligence findings and appeared to side with the Russian president. This moment sparked outrage in Washington, with critics accusing Trump of capitulating to Russian influence. Despite this, Trump insisted that better relations with Russia were in America's interest, arguing that diplomacy was preferable to confrontation.

However, while Trump's rhetoric was often favorable toward Putin, his administration pursued policies that directly challenged Russian interests. The U.S. imposed sanctions on Russian individuals and businesses in response to election interference, cyberattacks, and human rights violations. His administration also expelled dozens of Russian diplomats and provided military aid to Ukraine, a move that directly countered Russian expansionism. The Trump administration pressured European allies to reduce reliance on Russian energy by opposing the Nord Stream 2 pipeline, which would have strengthened Moscow's economic leverage over Europe. Despite these actions, Trump's reluctance to personally criticize Putin or acknowledge Russian aggression left many questioning whether his policies were driven by coercion, hidden interests, or an unconventional diplomatic strategy.

The ambiguity of the Trump-Putin relationship extended to global security issues, including arms control and military alliances. Trump withdrew the U.S. from the Intermediate-Range Nuclear Forces (INF) Treaty, citing Russian violations, further escalating tensions between the two nations. At the same time, his criticism of NATO and threats to reduce U.S. commitments to the alliance played into Putin's broader goal of weakening Western unity. Russia continued to assert its influence in Syria, Venezuela, and Libya, often in direct opposition to American interests, while Trump's administration responded with a mix of sanctions and diplomatic engagement.

Ultimately, the Trump-Putin dynamic remained one of the most perplexing aspects of Trump's foreign policy. While he sought to improve relations with Russia on the surface, his administration took numerous actions that challenged Russian interests. Whether Trump's admiration for Putin reflected a genuine effort at diplomacy or a reluctance to confront Russian aggression remains a matter of debate. What is clear is that the relationship between the two leaders reshaped global power dynamics, influencing everything from election security to military strategy in an increasingly polarized world.

Cyber Warfare and Election Interference

One of the most controversial aspects of U.S.-Russia relations during Donald Trump's presidency was the issue of cyber warfare and election interference. The rise of digital technology has transformed the landscape of geopolitical conflicts, with cyberattacks replacing traditional military confrontations as a key battleground.

Russia, under Vladimir Putin, has been widely accused of using cyber warfare as a strategic tool to undermine Western democracies, influence political outcomes, and destabilize global rivals. The 2016 U.S. presidential election was a turning point, as intelligence agencies confirmed that Russian operatives had engaged in a sophisticated campaign to influence American voters through hacking, disinformation, and social media manipulation. The Trump administration's response to these allegations was inconsistent, fueling suspicions about the nature of his relationship with Moscow and raising concerns about the future of election security in the digital age.

The Russian cyber interference in the 2016 election was conducted through a combination of hacking operations and disinformation campaigns. The hacking of the Democratic National Committee (DNC) and the email accounts of top Democratic officials led to the release of politically damaging information through platforms like WikiLeaks. These leaks fueled conspiracy theories and disrupted the Democratic campaign, playing into the broader strategy of sowing distrust in the American electoral process. Additionally, Russian troll farms and bot networks flooded social media with misleading content, fake news, and divisive rhetoric aimed at deepening political polarization in the U.S. Intelligence agencies, including the FBI, CIA, and NSA, concluded that these efforts were directed by the Russian government with the intention of helping Trump's candidacy while undermining public trust in democratic institutions.

Despite the overwhelming consensus among intelligence officials, Trump repeatedly downplayed the significance of Russian interference, often dismissing it as a hoax or attributing it to other actors, including China. His reluctance to acknowledge Moscow's role raised suspicions about his motivations, particularly during the infamous 2018 Helsinki summit, where he appeared to side with Putin over U.S. intelligence agencies. This stance caused significant backlash from both Republican and Democratic lawmakers, who viewed his position as a failure to confront a direct threat to American democracy. However, Trump's administration did impose sanctions on Russian individuals and organizations involved in election meddling, indicating a contradiction between his public rhetoric and official policy.

Beyond election interference, Russia continued to use cyber warfare to target critical infrastructure, businesses, and government agencies in the U.S. and its allies. Cyberattacks linked to Russian state-sponsored groups targeted everything from power grids and financial institutions to vaccine research during the COVID-19 pandemic. The SolarWinds hack, one of the most significant cyber espionage incidents in U.S. history, compromised multiple government agencies, including the Department of Defense and Homeland Security. While Trump's administration eventually acknowledged the attack, his initial response was muted, and he even suggested, without evidence, that China might be responsible. This lack of a strong and unified response raised concerns about America's ability to deter future cyber threats.

The rise of cyber warfare as a primary tool of geopolitical influence has reshaped the nature of modern conflict. Russia's success in leveraging digital tools to manipulate elections and disrupt governance has set a precedent for other nations, including China, Iran, and North Korea, to follow. The Trump administration's inconsistent approach to combating these threats left lingering vulnerabilities in U.S. cybersecurity, highlighting the urgent need for stronger defenses against digital warfare. As elections and governance become increasingly dependent on technology, securing democratic institutions from cyber interference will remain a crucial challenge for future administrations.

The Ukraine Crisis and NATO's Response

The Ukraine crisis has been a focal point of geopolitical tensions between Russia and the West for nearly a decade, and under the Trump administration, the conflict took on new dimensions. Since Russia's annexation of Crimea in 2014, Ukraine has been at the center of a broader struggle between Moscow's expansionist ambitions and NATO's efforts to counter Russian aggression. While previous U.S. administrations maintained a firm stance in supporting Ukraine against Russian incursions, Trump's approach was more inconsistent, oscillating between military aid and reluctance to confront Moscow directly. His administration provided lethal aid to Ukraine, but Trump's personal dealings with Ukrainian officials and his stance on NATO raised concerns about America's long-term commitment to European security.

One of the key aspects of Trump's Ukraine policy was his decision to provide military assistance to Kyiv. Unlike the Obama administration, which had limited U.S. support to non-lethal aid, Trump approved the sale of Javelin anti-tank missiles and other advanced weaponry to Ukraine, helping bolster its defenses against Russian-backed separatists in the Donbas region. This move was widely praised by foreign policy experts as a necessary step in deterring further Russian advances. However, Trump's support for Ukraine was overshadowed by his controversial dealings with Ukrainian officials, particularly his infamous phone call with President Volodymyr Zelensky, in which he pressured Ukraine to investigate Joe Biden's son, Hunter Biden. This episode led to

Trump's first impeachment in 2019, as critics accused him of leveraging military aid for political gain, damaging America's credibility as a reliable ally.

While the Trump administration provided military assistance to Ukraine, Trump's rhetoric on NATO and European security often undermined Western unity in responding to Russian aggression. Throughout his presidency, Trump repeatedly criticized NATO, calling it "obsolete" and threatening to withdraw the U.S. from the alliance unless member countries increased their defense spending. His stance caused anxiety among European allies, who viewed NATO as the primary deterrent against Russian expansionism. Although NATO remained committed to supporting Ukraine, Trump's mixed messages about the alliance's future created uncertainty, emboldening Russia's strategic position. Despite this, NATO took steps to strengthen its eastern flank by increasing troop deployments in Poland and the Baltic states, conducting military exercises, and enhancing coordination with Ukrainian forces.

The Ukraine crisis highlighted the broader struggle between Western democratic institutions and Russia's efforts to reassert its influence over former Soviet territories. While Trump's administration did take actions to counter Russia, including sanctions on Russian officials and companies involved in the Ukraine conflict, his personal admiration for Vladimir Putin raised concerns about his true commitment to standing up to Moscow. His reluctance to confront Putin directly—such as his failure to condemn Russian aggression during the Helsinki summit—sent mixed signals to both allies and adversaries. Meanwhile, Ukraine continued to resist Russian-backed forces with support from NATO and European partners, though the lack of a unified U.S. strategy made long-term solutions elusive.

By the end of Trump's presidency, the Ukraine crisis remained unresolved, with Russian-backed separatists still controlling parts of eastern Ukraine and tensions continuing to simmer. While NATO maintained its commitment to Ukraine's sovereignty, Trump's unpredictability and skepticism toward alliances weakened the West's collective response. The conflict underscored the growing challenge of countering Russian aggression while maintaining Western unity, a challenge that would continue to shape U.S. foreign policy beyond Trump's tenure.

Chapter 4
The Middle East: New Battles, Old Conflicts

The Middle East has long been a battleground for geopolitical struggles, and under Donald Trump's presidency, the region experienced both continuity and upheaval. While Trump campaigned on reducing U.S. involvement in foreign wars, his administration's policies in the Middle East often escalated tensions rather than diffusing them. He abandoned long-standing diplomatic agreements, strengthened ties with authoritarian regimes, and took an aggressive stance against Iran, shifting the balance of power in the region. Unlike his predecessors, who pursued strategies of engagement and containment, Trump's approach was driven by economic sanctions, military force, and transactional diplomacy. His administration's actions reshaped regional dynamics, leading to both historic agreements and renewed conflicts.

One of the defining aspects of Trump's Middle East policy was his unwavering support for Israel and Gulf Arab states while taking a hardline approach toward Iran. The withdrawal from the Iran Nuclear Deal (JCPOA) in 2018 marked a significant break from previous U.S. policy, reintroducing sanctions that crippled Iran's economy and escalated hostilities between Tehran and Washington. The Trump administration also brokered the Abraham Accords, normalizing relations between Israel and several Arab nations, a historic diplomatic breakthrough. However, these successes were overshadowed by growing instability, including the targeted assassination of Iranian General Qasem Soleimani, which pushed the region to the brink of war. Trump's unpredictable decision-making left both allies and adversaries uncertain about the long-term direction of U.S. involvement in the region.

Despite Trump's promise to end "endless wars," his administration struggled to navigate America's military presence in the Middle East. While he ordered troop withdrawals from Syria and Afghanistan, these decisions were often reversed or modified due to backlash from military leaders and allies. His sudden withdrawal of U.S. troops from northern Syria in 2019, for example, abandoned Kurdish allies who had been instrumental in the fight against ISIS, allowing Turkey to launch a military offensive against Kurdish forces. Meanwhile, his administration maintained a strong military presence in the Persian Gulf, reinforcing alliances with Saudi Arabia and the UAE. The Middle East remained a region of enduring conflict and shifting alliances, with Trump's policies deepening divisions and setting the stage for future instability.

The Abraham Accords and Their Unfinished Business

The Abraham Accords, signed during Donald Trump's presidency, marked a historic shift in Middle Eastern diplomacy. Brokered by the Trump administration in 2020, these agreements normalized relations between Israel and several Arab nations, including the United Arab Emirates (UAE), Bahrain, Sudan, and Morocco. The accords represented a breakthrough in Arab-Israeli relations, as they broke with decades of policy that conditioned normalization on a resolution to the Israeli-Palestinian conflict. While Trump hailed the agreements as a landmark achievement in diplomacy, the accords left several unresolved challenges, particularly regarding Palestinian statehood, regional security, and the long-term stability of the Middle East.

One of the key motivations behind the Abraham Accords was to counter Iran's growing influence in the region. The agreements solidified a new regional alliance between Israel and Sunni Arab states, particularly those that shared concerns over Iran's military and nuclear ambitions. By facilitating arms deals, economic partnerships, and intelligence-sharing between Israel and the Gulf nations, the Trump administration aimed to create a stronger front against Tehran. However, while the accords improved relations between signatory nations, they also deepened sectarian divides. Iran and its allies, including Hezbollah and Houthi rebels, condemned the agreements as a betrayal of the Palestinian cause, leading to increased tensions and continued proxy conflicts across the region.

Despite their diplomatic significance, the Abraham Accords did not address the core issue that has fueled Middle Eastern instability for decades—the Israeli-Palestinian conflict. The agreements largely sidelined the Palestinian leadership, who viewed them as a betrayal by Arab nations that had historically supported their cause. Palestinian leaders rejected the normalization process, arguing that it rewarded Israel while failing to secure concessions for Palestinian statehood. Trump's administration attempted to push forward a peace plan known as the Deal of the Century, but it was widely criticized as favoring Israel and failing to address key Palestinian demands. Without a meaningful resolution to the Palestinian issue, the Abraham Accords remain incomplete, with the potential for future conflicts to disrupt their fragile framework.

Beyond the Israeli-Palestinian question, the long-term success of the Abraham Accords depends on whether the new partnerships can withstand shifting political dynamics in both the U.S. and the Middle East. While the agreements have facilitated trade, tourism, and security cooperation, they remain vulnerable to changes in leadership and regional crises. The U.S. played a crucial role in brokering and enforcing these agreements, but with Trump's departure from office, questions arose about whether future administrations would continue prioritizing this diplomatic effort. Additionally, domestic politics in signatory countries could impact their commitment to normalization, particularly if opposition groups gain influence or public sentiment shifts against Israel.

Ultimately, while the Abraham Accords reshaped Middle Eastern diplomacy and fostered new alliances, their success remains incomplete without addressing deeper regional tensions. The agreements were a step toward greater cooperation, but they left unresolved issues that could threaten their durability. Moving forward, diplomatic efforts will need to focus not only on strengthening these new partnerships but also on addressing the underlying conflicts that continue to shape the region's future.

The Iran Nuclear Deal and Its Fallout

The Iran Nuclear Deal, formally known as the Joint Comprehensive Plan of Action (JCPOA), was one of the most significant and controversial international agreements of the 21st century. Signed in 2015 under the Obama administration, the deal was designed to curb Iran's nuclear program in exchange for sanctions relief. The agreement limited Iran's uranium enrichment, reduced its stockpile of nuclear materials, and subjected its facilities to international inspections. However, Donald Trump strongly opposed the JCPOA, labeling it a "terrible deal" that failed to address Iran's regional aggression and ballistic missile program. In 2018,

Trump announced the U.S. withdrawal from the agreement, reimposing sanctions and triggering a chain of events that escalated tensions between Washington and Tehran.

Trump's decision to exit the JCPOA was based on several key arguments. His administration claimed that the deal was too lenient on Iran, providing only temporary restrictions on its nuclear activities while failing to address its support for militant groups like Hezbollah, Hamas, and the Houthis. Additionally, the JCPOA did not restrict Iran's development of ballistic missiles, which posed a threat to U.S. allies in the Middle East. By reimposing harsh economic sanctions under a "maximum pressure" campaign, Trump sought to force Iran back to the negotiating table for a more comprehensive agreement. However, instead of bringing about a new deal, the withdrawal pushed Iran to retaliate by gradually abandoning its commitments under the JCPOA, reviving concerns about its nuclear ambitions.

The fallout from the withdrawal had far-reaching consequences, both in the Middle East and beyond. Economically, the reinstated U.S. sanctions devastated Iran's economy, reducing its oil exports, devaluing its currency, and increasing domestic unrest. However, rather than forcing Iran into submission, the sanctions pushed Tehran to take a more aggressive stance. Iran resumed uranium enrichment beyond the limits set by the JCPOA, stockpiling more nuclear material and reducing access for international inspectors. This development alarmed U.S. allies, particularly in Europe, who had worked to keep the agreement alive despite Washington's withdrawal. Countries such as France, Germany, and the UK tried to salvage the deal through diplomatic efforts, but Iran's escalating violations made it increasingly difficult to maintain.

Beyond the nuclear issue, U.S.-Iran tensions reached a boiling point in early 2020 when Trump ordered the assassination of General Qasem Soleimani, the commander of Iran's Quds Force. This move was justified by the administration as a response to Iranian-backed attacks on U.S. personnel in Iraq, but it significantly escalated hostilities between the two nations. Iran retaliated with missile strikes on U.S. bases in Iraq, bringing the two countries dangerously close to war. Meanwhile, Iranian-backed militias intensified their attacks on American assets in the Middle East, further destabilizing the region. The lack of a clear diplomatic pathway increased fears of a prolonged conflict, with both sides engaging in cyber warfare, proxy battles, and military posturing.

By the end of Trump's presidency, the Iran nuclear issue remained unresolved, with the region on edge and Tehran closer to developing nuclear capabilities than before. The U.S. withdrawal from the JCPOA did not achieve the intended goal of forcing a new agreement; instead, it exacerbated tensions and left a complex diplomatic challenge for future administrations. Whether a return to negotiations or further escalation would define U.S.-Iran relations remained an open question, but Trump's decision to abandon the deal undeniably reshaped the Middle East's geopolitical landscape.

U.S. Troop Withdrawals and Their Aftermath

One of Donald Trump's key foreign policy promises was to bring American troops home from prolonged military engagements, particularly in the Middle East and Afghanistan. Throughout his presidency, Trump criticized past U.S. interventions as costly and ineffective, arguing that America should no longer act as the world's "policeman." While he partially followed through on this pledge by reducing U.S. military presence in Afghanistan, Syria, and Iraq, the way these withdrawals were executed created instability, alienated allies, and in some cases, emboldened adversaries. Instead of ending conflicts, the troop withdrawals often left power vacuums that were quickly filled by hostile forces, undermining years of strategic efforts by the U.S. and its partners.

One of the most controversial troop withdrawals came in Syria in 2019, when Trump abruptly announced that U.S. forces would leave northern Syria, where they had been supporting Kurdish fighters in the battle against ISIS. The decision shocked U.S. military leaders and international allies, as the Kurdish-led Syrian Democratic Forces (SDF) had been America's most reliable partner in the fight against ISIS. Almost immediately after the withdrawal, Turkey launched a military offensive against Kurdish forces, seeing the pullout as an opportunity to push into northern Syria. The U.S. withdrawal effectively abandoned the Kurds, who had sacrificed thousands of fighters in the battle against ISIS, leading to widespread criticism that the U.S. had betrayed its allies. Additionally, the instability created by the withdrawal allowed ISIS to regroup in certain areas, raising concerns that the terror organization could regain strength.

In Afghanistan, Trump negotiated a deal with the Taliban in 2020, committing to a phased withdrawal of U.S. forces in exchange for Taliban assurances that they would prevent terrorist groups from using Afghan soil to launch attacks. This agreement, known as the Doha Agreement, paved the way for a complete U.S. exit, but it also signaled to the Taliban that the U.S. was eager to leave. As U.S. troops withdrew, the Taliban intensified their attacks on Afghan forces, capturing territory and preparing for a full takeover. Although the final withdrawal occurred under President Joe Biden in 2021, the foundation for the chaotic U.S. exit had been set during the Trump administration. The hasty troop reduction weakened the Afghan government and emboldened the Taliban, ultimately leading to the swift collapse of Kabul after the U.S. departure.

In Iraq, Trump also reduced the number of U.S. troops but maintained a limited presence to counter Iranian influence and prevent an ISIS resurgence. However, his administration's actions — particularly the assassination of Iranian General Qasem Soleimani in early 2020 — further inflamed tensions in the region. Iran-backed militias in Iraq ramped up attacks on U.S. forces and diplomatic facilities, forcing the Pentagon to keep some troops in place to safeguard American interests. While Trump aimed to reduce U.S. involvement in Middle Eastern conflicts, the reality was that strategic threats remained, making a full withdrawal difficult without jeopardizing regional stability.

Overall, Trump's approach to troop withdrawals reflected his desire to fulfill campaign promises, but the execution often led to unintended consequences. While reducing America's military footprint was a popular idea domestically, the manner in which withdrawals were conducted created chaos, weakened U.S. alliances, and left long-term security challenges unresolved. Instead of ending conflicts, these withdrawals often shifted power dynamics in ways that favored America's adversaries, raising concerns about the future of U.S. influence in global security affairs.

Chapter 5
The Rise of Populist Leaders and Nationalist Movements

The presidency of Donald Trump was not an isolated political phenomenon but part of a broader global trend that saw the rise of populist leaders and nationalist movements. Across the world, a new wave of politicians emerged, challenging traditional political establishments and appealing directly to the frustrations of ordinary citizens. These leaders, from Brazil's Jair Bolsonaro to Hungary's Viktor Orbán and India's Narendra Modi, leveraged nationalism, anti-elitism, and a promise to restore national pride to consolidate power. Trump's rise to the presidency mirrored this global shift, as he capitalized on economic anxieties, cultural divisions, and a rejection of globalism to redefine American politics. His influence extended beyond the U.S., emboldening nationalist leaders worldwide and reshaping global governance.

At the core of this populist surge was a rejection of traditional democratic institutions and multilateralism. Leaders like Trump and his international counterparts often portrayed the media, judiciary, and established political elites as obstacles to national progress. By positioning themselves as champions of the "forgotten people," they successfully mobilized large segments of the population who felt disillusioned with globalization, immigration, and economic inequality. Trump's policies, including his America First doctrine, reinforced the broader trend of nationalism, inspiring other leaders to prioritize their domestic agendas over international cooperation. This shift led to increased tensions between nations, as global agreements on trade, climate change, and human rights came under threat.

However, while populist leaders gained political power by promising to disrupt the status quo, their governance often led to polarization and institutional instability. Many of these leaders used divisive rhetoric to maintain their influence, deepening social and political divides within their countries. Trump's presidency saw unprecedented levels of political fragmentation in the U.S., culminating in events such as the January 6th Capitol riot. Similarly, nationalist movements in Europe and South America led to conflicts over immigration, press freedoms, and democratic norms. As these leaders pushed their countries toward more authoritarian governance styles, the global political landscape became increasingly volatile, raising concerns about the future of democracy and international stability.

Trump's Influence on Global Nationalism

Donald Trump's rise to power in 2016 was not just an American political event but a catalyst for a global surge in nationalist movements. His unapologetic embrace of nationalism, rejection of political correctness, and America First doctrine resonated with populist leaders across the world, inspiring a shift away from globalism and toward a more insular, country-first mindset. While nationalist movements had been gaining momentum before Trump, his presidency legitimized and reinforced these ideologies, providing a model for other leaders who sought to capitalize on public dissatisfaction with the political establishment. As a result, Trump's influence on global nationalism extended far beyond U.S. borders, reshaping the political landscape in Europe, Latin America, and Asia.

One of the most significant ways Trump influenced global nationalism was by challenging the post-World War II international order that emphasized multilateralism, free trade, and democratic cooperation. His administration's withdrawal from key agreements, such as the Paris Climate Accord and the Iran Nuclear Deal, sent a clear message that the U.S. would no longer prioritize international collaboration over national interests. This emboldened leaders like Brazil's Jair Bolsonaro, who mirrored Trump's rejection of environmental regulations, and Hungary's Viktor Orbán, who embraced anti-immigration policies and nationalism as core tenets of governance. Similarly, in the UK, the Brexit movement, which gained traction around the same time as Trump's election, echoed his rhetoric of reclaiming national sovereignty and reducing dependence on foreign entities like the European Union.

Beyond policy decisions, Trump's style of leadership also had a profound impact on nationalist movements worldwide. His frequent attacks on the media, judiciary, and political elites reinforced the idea that traditional institutions were obstacles to progress. This inspired other leaders, such as India's Narendra Modi and the Philippines' Rodrigo Duterte, to adopt similar tactics, positioning themselves as representatives of the "real people" against corrupt elites. Trump's success in using social media to bypass traditional news outlets and speak directly to his supporters also became a model for other nationalist leaders, who embraced platforms like Twitter and Facebook to rally their base, spread nationalist rhetoric, and challenge mainstream narratives.

However, while Trump's influence strengthened nationalist movements, it also deepened divisions within and between nations. His presidency saw an increase in political polarization, not only in the U.S. but globally, as nationalist leaders used his tactics to marginalize opposition, restrict press freedoms, and consolidate power. In some cases, this led to direct confrontations between nationalist and globalist forces, such as protests in Brazil against Bolsonaro's policies, pro-democracy movements in Hungary, and civil unrest in India over religious nationalism. Additionally, Trump's rhetoric on immigration, race, and foreign relations provided justification for policies that marginalized minority groups, increased xenophobia, and intensified social tensions.

By the time Trump left office, the nationalist wave he had helped amplify was still gaining momentum. While some nationalist leaders, like Bolsonaro, faced political setbacks, others, such as Orbán and Modi, continued to expand their influence. The long-term impact of Trump's nationalist approach remains uncertain, but his presidency undeniably reshaped global politics by proving that nationalism could be a winning strategy in the modern era. Whether future leaders will sustain this movement or face backlash from increasingly polarized societies remains one of the key questions in the evolving landscape of global governance.

Strongmen Politics: From Bolsonaro to Modi

The rise of Donald Trump was not an isolated political event but part of a global trend toward strongmen politics, where leaders consolidate power by appealing to nationalism, rejecting traditional democratic institutions, and positioning themselves as defenders of the "real people" against corrupt elites. Trump's leadership style, characterized by direct attacks on the media, courts, and political opponents, emboldened leaders around the world to adopt similar tactics. Figures like Jair Bolsonaro in Brazil, Viktor Orbán in Hungary, Narendra Modi in India, and Rodrigo Duterte in the Philippines all embraced variations of strongman governance, using populist rhetoric, nationalism, and authoritarian tendencies to secure power. Their leadership reshaped the global political landscape, intensifying divisions and raising concerns about the future of democracy.

One of the most striking examples of Trump's influence on strongmen politics was Brazilian President Jair Bolsonaro, often referred to as the "Trump of the Tropics." Bolsonaro, like Trump, dismissed climate change concerns, attacked the media, and championed an anti-globalist, nationalist agenda. He downplayed the COVID-19 pandemic, spread misinformation, and frequently used social media to rally his base while dismissing traditional news outlets as biased. His government also promoted policies that favored big business and deforestation in the Amazon, mirroring Trump's rollback of environmental regulations in the U.S. Bolsonaro's refusal to accept electoral defeat in 2022 further mirrored Trump's baseless claims of election fraud, demonstrating the broader impact of Trump-style politics on democratic institutions worldwide.

In India, Narendra Modi embodied strongman politics by blending Hindu nationalism with economic populism. Modi, a powerful orator, positioned himself as a defender of Hindu identity, appealing to the country's majority population while marginalizing religious minorities, particularly Muslims. His government implemented policies such as the Citizenship Amendment Act (CAA) and the revocation of Article 370 in Kashmir, which were widely seen as targeting Muslim communities. Modi, like Trump, thrived on a cult of personality, using mass rallies, social media campaigns, and direct appeals to national pride to solidify his support. His government also cracked down on dissent, with journalists and activists facing increasing pressure, echoing the tactics used by other nationalist leaders to suppress opposition.

Hungary's Viktor Orbán and the Philippines' Rodrigo Duterte also followed the strongman model, taking extreme measures to control political discourse. Orbán systematically weakened Hungary's democratic institutions by reshaping the judiciary, limiting press freedom, and consolidating power under his ruling party. Duterte, known for his brutal war on drugs, encouraged extrajudicial killings and publicly dismissed human rights concerns, adopting a tough-guy image similar to Trump's law-and-order rhetoric. Both leaders used fear-based narratives to justify authoritarian policies, demonstrating how strongmen leaders manipulate public anxieties to maintain control.

While strongman politics has proven effective in securing power, it has also deepened political polarization, weakened democratic institutions, and increased authoritarian tendencies across the world. Leaders like Trump, Bolsonaro, Modi, Orbán, and Duterte have shown how nationalist and populist rhetoric can be weaponized to dismantle checks and balances. However, resistance movements, mass protests, and electoral defeats have also demonstrated that strongman politics is not invincible. As global politics continues to evolve, the battle between authoritarian nationalism and democratic resilience remains one of the defining struggles of the modern era.

The Erosion of Democratic Institutions

The rise of populist leaders like Donald Trump, Jair Bolsonaro, Viktor Orbán, and Narendra Modi has coincided with a global trend of democratic backsliding. These leaders, often elected through democratic means, have systematically weakened institutions designed to uphold checks and balances, protect free speech, and ensure fair governance. The erosion of democratic institutions is not always achieved through outright authoritarianism but through gradual changes—manipulating judicial systems, controlling the media, weakening electoral oversight, and undermining trust in democratic processes. While this phenomenon is not unique to Trump's presidency, his approach to governance set a precedent for other nationalist leaders to challenge democratic norms while maintaining a facade of legitimacy.

One of the most concerning aspects of democratic erosion is the undermining of judicial independence. In many countries where populist leaders have risen to power, courts have faced increasing political pressure. In the U.S., Trump sought to reshape the judiciary by appointing conservative judges at an unprecedented rate, ensuring that legal decisions aligned with his administration's agenda. While judicial appointments are a routine part of governance, Trump often attacked judges who ruled against him, calling them "biased" or "activist" and questioning their legitimacy. This pattern was mirrored in other countries—Orbán in Hungary and Modi in India systematically reduced judicial independence, appointing loyalists to courts and making it difficult for legal challenges against government policies to succeed.

Another major factor contributing to the decline of democratic institutions is the manipulation of the electoral process. Trump's repeated claims of voter fraud, despite no substantial evidence, significantly eroded public trust in U.S. elections. His refusal to accept the results of the 2020 presidential election led to the January 6th Capitol riot, a direct attack on democratic institutions. Similar tactics were used by Bolsonaro in Brazil, who sowed doubt about electronic voting before his electoral defeat in 2022, and by Orbán, who changed electoral laws to favor his ruling party. In many cases, these leaders have worked to suppress voter participation through restrictive voting laws, gerrymandering, or misinformation campaigns designed to discredit electoral processes.

Another key tactic in the erosion of democracy is the restriction of press freedom and the silencing of dissent. Trump's frequent attacks on the media as the "enemy of the people" set a dangerous precedent, encouraging other strongmen leaders to dismiss unfavorable reporting as "fake news." In countries like India, Hungary, and Turkey, governments have taken this strategy even further by imprisoning journalists, shutting down independent media outlets, and passing laws that criminalize dissent. The result is an environment where governments can operate with less scrutiny, reducing transparency and accountability.

Beyond formal institutions, democratic norms have also deteriorated as populist leaders have deepened political polarization and used identity politics to consolidate power. By framing politics as a battle between "the people" and "the elites" or between nationalists and perceived outsiders, these leaders have created divisions that weaken democratic cohesion. Trump's rhetoric on immigration, race, and globalism, for example, fueled social conflicts that made bipartisan governance increasingly difficult. In countries like Brazil and India, similar narratives have been used to justify crackdowns on political opposition and minority communities.

The erosion of democratic institutions is not an overnight process but a slow and deliberate effort to weaken the foundations of accountability, free speech, and fair governance. While strongmen leaders justify these actions as necessary to protect national interests, the long-term consequences threaten to undermine democratic values worldwide. Whether these institutions can withstand such assaults or whether democracy will continue to decline depends on the resilience of civil society, the media, and the willingness of the public to defend their rights against authoritarian tendencies.

Chapter 6
Cyber Warfare: The New Battlefield

The rise of cyber warfare has transformed the nature of global conflict, shifting battles from traditional military engagements to digital arenas where nations, corporations, and individuals are vulnerable to unseen attacks. Unlike conventional warfare, cyber warfare is asymmetric, allowing state and non-state actors to target critical infrastructure, disrupt economies, and manipulate political systems without deploying soldiers or weapons. During Trump's presidency, the growing reliance on technology and the internet made cyber threats more dangerous than ever, with state-sponsored hacking, election interference, and cyber espionage becoming key tools in geopolitical rivalries. The United States, Russia, China, Iran, and North Korea were among the primary players in this new battlefield, engaging in cyberattacks that reshaped global security concerns.

Under Trump, the U.S. faced some of the most significant cyber threats in its history, including election interference, data breaches, and infrastructure attacks. Russian operatives conducted disinformation campaigns to manipulate public opinion, while Chinese hackers targeted intellectual property and sensitive government data. One of the most high-profile incidents was the SolarWinds cyberattack, in which Russian-linked hackers infiltrated U.S. government agencies, defense contractors, and Fortune 500 companies, exposing vulnerabilities in national cybersecurity. Meanwhile, Iran and North Korea engaged in cyberattacks against financial institutions and energy infrastructure, demonstrating that cyber warfare was no longer limited to great-power conflicts but was being used by smaller nations as well.

While cyber warfare presented new threats, Trump's administration had a mixed approach to cybersecurity, often downplaying the severity of cyberattacks while simultaneously investing in offensive cyber capabilities. His administration strengthened U.S. Cyber Command and launched cyber operations against adversaries, including disabling Iranian cyber networks following attacks on Saudi oil facilities. However, Trump's skepticism toward intelligence agencies and his reluctance to acknowledge Russian cyber activities weakened America's ability to build a coordinated response. The lack of a unified cybersecurity strategy left many vulnerabilities unaddressed, raising concerns about how prepared the U.S. and its allies were for future cyber conflicts. As cyber warfare continues to evolve, nations must adapt to the growing reality that future wars will not only be fought with missiles and troops but also through algorithms, digital espionage, and cyber sabotage.

Disinformation Campaigns and Digital Propaganda

The digital age has revolutionized how information is created, shared, and consumed. While this has fostered global connectivity, it has also enabled the rise of disinformation campaigns and digital propaganda, tools that have become central to modern cyber warfare. Governments, intelligence agencies, and political groups now use social media platforms, online news sources, and artificial intelligence to manipulate public opinion, spread false narratives, and undermine democratic institutions. During Donald Trump's presidency, disinformation became a critical weapon in both domestic and international conflicts, with state actors like Russia, China, and Iran using digital propaganda to influence elections, create social divisions, and shape global perceptions.

One of the most infamous examples of disinformation warfare was Russia's interference in the 2016 U.S. presidential election, a campaign designed to manipulate American voters and sow distrust in democratic institutions. Russian operatives, primarily through the Internet Research Agency (IRA), created thousands of fake social media accounts posing as American citizens, spreading politically divisive content to exacerbate racial, ideological, and cultural tensions. These accounts promoted false news stories, conspiracy theories, and misleading narratives, targeting both conservative and liberal audiences to deepen polarization. Russian hackers also infiltrated the Democratic National Committee (DNC), leaking sensitive emails that fueled political controversies. The goal was not necessarily to support Trump outright but to erode public trust in the electoral system, making American democracy appear chaotic and vulnerable.

China and Iran also engaged in digital propaganda operations, each with its own strategic objectives. China's cyber units focused on controlling the narrative around its global influence, particularly in relation to Taiwan, Hong Kong, and human rights violations in Xinjiang. Chinese state-controlled media and bot networks spread messages defending Beijing's policies while attacking Western criticisms, often labeling dissent as foreign interference. Similarly, Iran launched digital propaganda campaigns targeting U.S. foreign policy, amplifying anti-American sentiment and criticizing Trump's decisions, particularly regarding the Iran Nuclear Deal withdrawal and the assassination of General Qasem Soleimani. These campaigns used fake news sites, social media bots, and coordinated influence operations to shape public perception in both the U.S. and the Middle East.

While foreign disinformation efforts were a major concern, domestic digital propaganda also played a significant role in shaping political discourse during Trump's presidency. Trump himself frequently labeled unfavorable media coverage as "fake news", a tactic that blurred the line between factual reporting and political spin. His administration and allies used social media platforms like Twitter and Facebook to bypass traditional news outlets, spreading unverified claims about voter fraud, COVID-19, and political opponents. The rapid spread of conspiracy theories, such as QAnon, demonstrated how disinformation could move from fringe internet forums to mainstream political discussions, influencing millions of people.

The impact of disinformation and digital propaganda is profound, leading to increased polarization, erosion of trust in institutions, and destabilization of democracies. The challenge for future governments is not only to combat foreign interference but also to address the internal vulnerabilities that allow misinformation to thrive. With the rise of deepfake technology, AI-generated news, and automated bot networks, digital disinformation will continue to evolve, making it an ever-present threat in the cyber warfare landscape. The battle for truth is no longer just about journalistic integrity—it has become a key front in the fight for political stability and global influence.

The Role of AI and Cybersecurity in Modern Warfare

The rapid advancements in artificial intelligence (AI) and cybersecurity have fundamentally changed the landscape of modern warfare. No longer confined to traditional battlefields, conflicts are now waged in the digital domain, where AI-driven systems and cyber operations play an increasingly dominant role. Governments, intelligence agencies, and military organizations across the world are integrating AI into their defense strategies, using it for autonomous weapons, cyber defense, and intelligence gathering. Meanwhile, the rise of cyber threats has made cybersecurity a national security priority, with countries investing heavily in protective measures to safeguard critical infrastructure, sensitive data, and military networks. As warfare continues to evolve, AI and cybersecurity have become key components in shaping the future of global conflicts.

One of the most significant applications of AI in warfare is its use in autonomous weapon systems and military decision-making. AI-powered drones, for example, can conduct surveillance, execute precision strikes, and operate in hostile environments with minimal human intervention. These autonomous systems provide a strategic advantage by reducing the risk to human soldiers while increasing the efficiency of military operations. Additionally, AI is being used in predictive analytics, helping military leaders analyze vast amounts of data to anticipate enemy movements, detect cyber threats, and optimize battlefield strategies. AI-driven simulations and war games also allow defense departments to test scenarios and refine their response strategies before actual conflicts arise. However, the growing reliance on AI in warfare raises ethical concerns, particularly regarding the lack of human oversight in life-or-death decisions and the potential for AI-driven weapons to be used in unregulated combat scenarios.

Cybersecurity has also become an essential element of modern warfare, as cyberattacks have replaced traditional acts of aggression in many conflicts. Governments and militaries are increasingly vulnerable to cyber warfare tactics such as hacking, data breaches, and ransomware attacks. State-sponsored cyber operations from countries like Russia, China, Iran, and North Korea have targeted everything from power grids and banking systems to military installations and election infrastructure. One of the most notorious cyberattacks in recent history was the SolarWinds hack, in which Russian hackers infiltrated multiple U.S. government agencies, compromising sensitive national security data. Such attacks highlight the growing need for robust cyber defenses, as a single breach can cause widespread disruption, economic damage, and even compromise military operations.

The integration of AI into cybersecurity has enhanced defensive capabilities, allowing for real-time threat detection, automated responses, and adaptive security measures that can counter cyber threats before they escalate. AI-powered cybersecurity systems can analyze vast amounts of data, identify suspicious patterns, and neutralize potential threats faster than human analysts. However, the same AI advancements that strengthen cyber defenses can also be weaponized by adversaries. AI-driven cyberattacks can generate sophisticated malware, conduct large-scale phishing campaigns, and even manipulate digital communications to spread disinformation. As AI continues to evolve, the race between cyber offense and cyber defense will intensify, requiring nations to stay ahead of rapidly advancing threats.

In the modern era, AI and cybersecurity are no longer just tools for defense—they are weapons in their own right. The increasing use of AI-driven warfare and cyber operations has blurred the lines between physical and digital battlefields, making cyber resilience a crucial component of national security. As technology continues to advance, governments must invest in AI governance, cybersecurity frameworks, and international regulations to prevent conflicts from escalating into autonomous and cyber-driven warfare. The future of warfare will not just be fought with guns and missiles but with algorithms, machine learning, and digital fortifications.

The Growing Threat of Cyberterrorism

As technology continues to evolve, cyberterrorism has emerged as one of the most significant threats to global security. Unlike traditional terrorism, which relies on physical attacks, cyberterrorism uses digital means to disrupt critical infrastructure, spread fear, and destabilize societies. Terrorist organizations and extremist groups are increasingly leveraging cyber warfare tactics to target governments, corporations, and individuals, making cybersecurity a key battleground in modern conflict. With the expansion of artificial intelligence (AI), the Internet of Things (IoT), and digital connectivity, cyberterrorism is becoming more sophisticated, enabling attackers to launch devastating cyberattacks without ever stepping onto a physical battlefield.

One of the most alarming aspects of cyberterrorism is its potential to cripple essential services and infrastructure. Power grids, water supplies, hospitals, and financial systems are all vulnerable to cyberattacks that could cause widespread disruption. A well-executed cyberattack on a country's energy sector, for instance, could shut down electricity for millions, creating chaos and economic paralysis. In 2015, Russian hackers targeted Ukraine's power grid, leaving over 200,000 people without electricity—an attack that demonstrated how cyberterrorism could be weaponized in modern warfare. Similar threats loom over other nations, with experts warning that cyberterrorist groups could exploit vulnerabilities in smart grids, transportation networks, and emergency response systems to inflict maximum damage.

Beyond infrastructure, cyberterrorism plays a significant role in propaganda and radicalization. Terrorist organizations like ISIS have effectively used the internet to spread extremist ideologies, recruit followers, and coordinate attacks. Encrypted messaging apps, social media platforms, and dark web forums provide cyberterrorists with a global reach, allowing them to operate in secrecy while influencing individuals worldwide. AI-generated deepfake videos and manipulated digital content can amplify misinformation, creating confusion and increasing radicalization efforts. This digital warfare has made it increasingly difficult for intelligence agencies to track and disrupt terrorist networks, as cyberterrorists continuously adapt to new technologies and evasion techniques.

Another growing concern is the use of ransomware and cyber extortion by terrorist groups. Unlike state-sponsored cyberattacks, which are often politically motivated, cyberterrorists may seek financial gain by infiltrating corporate or government networks and demanding ransom payments. Ransomware attacks, such as the WannaCry and Colonial Pipeline incidents, demonstrated how cybercriminals could cripple essential services and demand millions in cryptocurrency in exchange for restoring access. While these attacks have primarily been carried out by financially motivated hackers, terrorist organizations are increasingly adopting similar tactics to fund their operations, posing a dual threat of financial and operational disruption.

Governments and cybersecurity experts are working to counter these threats by strengthening cyber defenses, increasing intelligence-sharing, and developing AI-powered cybersecurity tools to detect and neutralize cyberterrorist activities. However, as technology continues to advance, so do the capabilities of cyberterrorists. The future of warfare will not only involve physical counterterrorism efforts but also digital countermeasures designed to prevent cyberattacks before they occur. As nations grapple with these new security challenges, it is clear that cyberterrorism represents a growing and evolving threat that demands urgent and continuous attention. The battle against cyberterrorism is no longer confined to conventional military engagements but has extended into the digital world, where the consequences of a single cyberattack could be just as devastating as a traditional act of terrorism.

Chapter 7
The Global Economy: Trade Wars and Economic Showdowns

The global economy underwent significant upheaval during Donald Trump's presidency, as his administration pursued aggressive trade policies that reshaped international economic relations. By embracing protectionism and rejecting multilateral trade agreements, Trump initiated a series of trade wars, most notably with China, but also with key U.S. allies in Europe and North America. His belief that past trade agreements had disadvantaged the United States led to a wave of tariffs, renegotiations, and economic sanctions, disrupting supply chains and straining diplomatic ties. These actions not only impacted global markets but also set the stage for a more fragmented and competitive economic landscape, where nations prioritized national interests over economic cooperation.

The most consequential trade war under Trump was the U.S.-China economic confrontation, which saw both nations imposing retaliatory tariffs on hundreds of billions of dollars' worth of goods. This trade dispute disrupted global manufacturing and supply chains, affecting industries from technology to agriculture. While the Trump administration aimed to reduce America's trade deficit and curb China's economic influence, the result was economic uncertainty, increased costs for businesses and consumers, and slower global growth. Other trade battles, including disputes with Canada, Mexico, and the European Union, further underscored Trump's willingness to challenge long-standing economic partnerships in pursuit of what he saw as fairer deals for American workers and industries.

Beyond trade wars, Trump's economic policies also had wider geopolitical implications, influencing energy markets, financial regulations, and global investment flows. Sanctions against countries like Iran and Venezuela reshaped the oil industry, while the U.S.-Mexico-Canada Agreement (USMCA) replaced NAFTA, reflecting a shift toward bilateral and regional agreements over multilateral trade pacts. The economic impact of these policies was further complicated by the COVID-19 pandemic, which exposed vulnerabilities in global trade networks and forced governments to rethink economic dependencies. As the world adapted to these disruptions, Trump's economic legacy remained a subject of debate, with some viewing his policies as necessary corrections to flawed trade relationships, while others criticized them for destabilizing global commerce and increasing tensions among economic superpowers.

Tariffs, Sanctions, and the Cost of Economic Wars

Donald Trump's presidency was marked by an aggressive approach to economic policy, using tariffs and sanctions as key weapons in what he saw as a necessary battle to reshape global trade. His administration pursued a strategy of economic nationalism, arguing that past trade agreements and globalization had weakened American industries and cost domestic jobs. By imposing tariffs on foreign goods, renegotiating trade agreements, and placing economic sanctions on adversarial nations, Trump aimed to reassert U.S.

dominance in the global economy. However, these economic wars came at a cost, leading to disruptions in global supply chains, retaliatory measures from affected nations, and financial strain on American consumers and businesses.

One of the most significant aspects of Trump's economic warfare was his tariff policy, particularly in the U.S.-China trade war. In 2018, the administration imposed tariffs on over $360 billion worth of Chinese imports, targeting industries such as steel, electronics, and consumer goods. The goal was to force China to change its trade practices, particularly regarding intellectual property theft and unfair subsidies to state-owned enterprises. China retaliated with tariffs of its own, hitting American agricultural exports, automotive industries, and technology firms. The tit-for-tat trade war caused global market volatility, increased costs for manufacturers and consumers, and slowed economic growth in both countries. While Trump claimed that tariffs would boost American manufacturing, many businesses struggled with higher production costs, and farmers faced steep losses due to declining exports.

Beyond tariffs, economic sanctions became a central tool of Trump's foreign policy, targeting countries such as Iran, Venezuela, Russia, and North Korea. The reimposition of sanctions on Iran following the U.S. withdrawal from the Joint Comprehensive Plan of Action (JCPOA) was particularly impactful, crippling Iran's economy by cutting off its access to international markets and reducing its oil exports. While the sanctions were intended to pressure Tehran into renegotiating a stricter nuclear deal, they also deepened tensions in the Middle East, leading to military confrontations and increased instability. Similarly, sanctions on Venezuela's oil industry and financial sector weakened Nicolás Maduro's government but also worsened the country's humanitarian crisis, affecting millions of Venezuelans.

Trump also used sanctions against Russia, particularly in response to election interference, cyberattacks, and geopolitical aggression in Ukraine. However, his administration's approach to Russia was often contradictory—while the U.S. imposed financial and travel restrictions on Russian oligarchs and businesses, Trump himself frequently expressed admiration for Vladimir Putin and sought to improve U.S.-Russia relations. This inconsistency in enforcement and rhetoric created uncertainty about the effectiveness of sanctions in deterring Russian actions.

Despite Trump's claims that his economic wars were benefiting the U.S., the reality was more complex. Tariffs led to higher prices for consumers, trade disputes hurt American farmers and exporters, and sanctions sometimes had unintended humanitarian consequences. While some industries did benefit from protectionist measures, the overall impact of Trump's tariff and sanction policies remains debated. Supporters argue that his approach was necessary to counter unfair trade practices and economic coercion by rival nations, while critics contend that his isolationist policies harmed global economic stability and weakened long-standing alliances. Ultimately, the economic wars initiated under Trump reshaped international trade, but they also left behind challenges that future administrations would have to navigate.

The Weaponization of the U.S. Dollar

The U.S. dollar has long been the world's dominant reserve currency, playing a central role in global trade, finance, and economic stability. However, under Donald Trump's presidency, the dollar was increasingly weaponized as a tool of economic warfare, used to exert pressure on adversarial nations and enforce U.S. geopolitical interests. By leveraging the dollar's global influence, Trump's administration implemented sweeping economic sanctions, trade restrictions, and financial blacklisting, forcing countries to comply with U.S. foreign policy objectives. While this strategy proved effective in the short term, it also pushed rival nations to seek alternatives to the dollar, raising concerns about the long-term consequences of financial coercion.

One of the most significant ways Trump weaponized the dollar was through economic sanctions, which targeted countries such as Iran, Venezuela, Russia, North Korea, and China. These sanctions restricted access to the U.S. financial system, effectively freezing assets, blocking transactions, and cutting off trade relationships. The most notable case was Iran, which faced severe economic hardship after the U.S. withdrew from the Joint Comprehensive Plan of Action (JCPOA) and reinstated sanctions. These measures crippled Iran's oil exports, devalued its currency, and isolated it from global markets, forcing Tehran into economic turmoil. Similarly, Venezuela's oil-dependent economy collapsed under U.S. sanctions, leading to severe inflation, food shortages, and mass migration. By denying targeted nations access to the dollar, the Trump administration was able to exert economic pressure without direct military intervention.

Another key component of dollar weaponization was financial blacklisting, in which the U.S. used its control over global banking networks to restrict financial transactions involving sanctioned entities. The SWIFT (Society for Worldwide Interbank Financial Telecommunication) system, which facilitates international payments, became a powerful tool in this strategy. The U.S. pressured SWIFT to disconnect Iranian banks, making it nearly impossible for Iran to conduct trade in dollars. Additionally, secondary sanctions were imposed on foreign companies that engaged in business with sanctioned countries, effectively forcing multinational corporations and financial institutions to choose between doing business with the U.S. or with targeted nations. This extraterritorial reach made the dollar a formidable instrument of economic control, reinforcing U.S. dominance in global finance.

However, the aggressive use of the dollar as a weapon also triggered a global push for de-dollarization, as affected nations sought alternatives to bypass U.S. financial control. China, Russia, Iran, and other countries began developing new payment systems, trade agreements, and digital currencies to reduce reliance on the dollar. China's Belt and Road Initiative (BRI) promoted trade in yuan, while Russia expanded its use of the euro and gold reserves. Additionally, cryptocurrencies and central bank digital currencies (CBDCs) gained traction as potential alternatives to the dollar-based financial system. These efforts signaled a shift toward a multipolar economic order, where nations sought to reduce their vulnerability to U.S. financial coercion.

While the weaponization of the U.S. dollar provided Trump with a powerful tool to exert pressure on global adversaries, it also accelerated the fragmentation of the global financial system. By overusing economic sanctions and financial restrictions, the U.S. risked diminishing the long-term dominance of the dollar, as more nations explored alternative trade and financial networks. The future of American economic power will depend on whether the dollar remains the undisputed currency of global trade or whether the increasing push for de-dollarization reshapes the financial landscape in the years to come.

China's Belt and Road Initiative vs. Trump's Isolationism

China's Belt and Road Initiative (BRI) and Donald Trump's America First isolationism represented two vastly different approaches to global economic strategy, shaping international relations and trade policies in profound ways. While China aggressively expanded its influence by investing in infrastructure and building economic partnerships across multiple continents, Trump's administration focused on withdrawing from multilateral trade agreements, prioritizing domestic industries, and reshaping U.S. foreign trade policies through tariffs and sanctions. These competing approaches reflected not only different economic priorities but also contrasting visions for global leadership, with China positioning itself as the world's economic engine while the U.S. pursued a more nationalist, self-reliant path.

China's BRI, launched in 2013 by President Xi Jinping, was a massive global initiative designed to connect markets across Asia, Africa, Europe, and Latin America through infrastructure development. By funding roads, railways, ports, and telecommunications projects, China sought to integrate global economies under its economic influence, offering an alternative to the U.S.-led financial system. While many developing nations welcomed Chinese investments as a means to modernize their economies, critics warned that these projects often came with significant debt burdens, leading to concerns about Beijing using financial leverage to exert political control. The initiative reinforced China's role as a dominant force in global trade, strengthening its economic ties with emerging markets and positioning itself as a key driver of global growth.

Meanwhile, Trump's administration pursued a starkly different approach, favoring economic nationalism over global integration. His withdrawal from the Trans-Pacific Partnership (TPP), a trade deal designed to counterbalance China's influence in Asia, left a vacuum that Beijing quickly exploited by strengthening its trade relationships through agreements like the Regional Comprehensive Economic Partnership (RCEP). Trump's skepticism toward international institutions, including the World Trade Organization (WTO) and NATO, further signaled America's retreat from multilateral engagement. Instead of relying on trade agreements and diplomatic economic policies, Trump favored tariffs as a primary tool to reshape global trade dynamics, engaging in a prolonged trade war with China. While his administration claimed these tariffs were necessary to correct long-standing trade imbalances and protect American jobs, the result was increased costs for businesses, supply chain disruptions, and retaliatory tariffs that hurt American farmers and exporters.

The contrast between China's expansionist economic strategy and Trump's isolationism had significant geopolitical consequences. As the U.S. withdrew from major trade negotiations and imposed economic barriers, many countries that traditionally aligned with American economic policies turned to China as a more stable trading partner. China capitalized on this shift, expanding its reach in Africa, Latin America, and Southeast Asia, where countries saw the BRI as a crucial avenue for economic development. The U.S., on the other hand, found itself increasingly isolated, as its traditional allies were forced to navigate a global economy where China played an ever-growing role.

The long-term effects of these opposing strategies remain to be seen. While Trump's policies were designed to prioritize American economic strength and reduce reliance on foreign manufacturing, they also alienated global partners and weakened U.S. influence in international trade. China's BRI, despite its success in expanding Beijing's economic reach, has also faced challenges, including debt sustainability issues and geopolitical resistance from nations wary of Chinese dominance. As global economic power continues to shift, the competition between these two approaches will shape the future of international trade and geopolitical alliances, determining whether global integration or economic nationalism becomes the dominant force in the decades ahead.

Chapter 8
The Role of the Military-Industrial Complex

The military-industrial complex has long been a driving force in shaping U.S. foreign policy, influencing military strategies, defense spending, and geopolitical conflicts. Under Donald Trump's presidency, this relationship between the government, defense contractors, and military institutions remained strong, despite his early campaign promises to reduce America's involvement in foreign wars. Trump positioned himself as an outsider who would challenge the status quo, criticizing costly military interventions and advocating for a more restrained foreign policy. However, in practice, his administration significantly increased defense spending, expanded arms deals, and maintained America's global military presence, reinforcing the influence of the military-industrial complex rather than diminishing it.

A key feature of Trump's approach was the record-high defense budgets, which prioritized the modernization of the U.S. military while benefiting major defense contractors like Lockheed Martin, Boeing, and Raytheon. His administration secured massive arms deals, particularly with Saudi Arabia, despite mounting international criticism over human rights abuses and the war in Yemen. Trump justified these sales by emphasizing economic benefits and job creation in the defense sector, further entrenching the military-industrial complex as a cornerstone of his economic strategy. While he sought to reduce direct military engagements in regions like the Middle East, his policies relied on increased arms sales, military partnerships, and private defense contracts to sustain U.S. influence without deploying large numbers of troops.

Despite Trump's rhetoric about ending "endless wars," his administration's actions often contradicted this promise, as military interventions, drone strikes, and covert operations continued across multiple regions. His escalatory stance toward Iran, highlighted by the assassination of General Qasem Soleimani, demonstrated how deeply embedded military strategies remained in U.S. foreign policy. Furthermore, the administration's withdrawal from treaties such as the Intermediate-Range Nuclear Forces (INF) Treaty fueled concerns about a renewed arms race, signaling that military dominance remained a priority. The military-industrial complex thrived under Trump, not through traditional large-scale wars but through expanded arms sales, increased defense budgets, and continued geopolitical tensions, ensuring its lasting influence on U.S. policy for years to come.

Increased Defense Spending and the Arms Race

Donald Trump's presidency saw a significant increase in U.S. defense spending, reinforcing the power of the military-industrial complex while intensifying global competition in military capabilities. Despite his campaign promises to reduce America's involvement in foreign wars, Trump's administration approved record-high defense budgets, arguing that a stronger military was necessary for maintaining U.S. dominance and countering emerging threats from China, Russia, and Iran. This surge in defense spending not only benefited major arms manufacturers but also signaled a shift toward a modernized arms race, where nations prioritized military expansion and technological advancements over diplomatic solutions.

One of the defining aspects of Trump's defense policy was massive military funding increases, with the Pentagon's budget surpassing $700 billion annually. This funding was directed toward developing new weapon systems, expanding nuclear capabilities, and enhancing military readiness. A significant portion of this budget went to modernizing the U.S. nuclear arsenal, including upgrading intercontinental ballistic missiles (ICBMs), building new nuclear submarines, and revamping strategic bombers. The administration also pushed for the development of hypersonic weapons and space-based defense systems, emphasizing the need to stay ahead of competitors like China and Russia. Trump's creation of the U.S. Space Force as an independent military branch underscored the administration's focus on militarizing space, adding a new dimension to the global arms race.

Beyond domestic military expansion, Trump also prioritized arms sales to foreign nations, arguing that these deals would boost the U.S. economy and create jobs. His administration approved billions of dollars in arms sales to Saudi Arabia, the United Arab Emirates, and other allies, despite concerns over human rights violations and regional instability. The 2018 $110 billion arms deal with Saudi Arabia was one of the largest in history, supplying fighter jets, missiles, and other military equipment to the kingdom. These sales not only strengthened U.S. defense companies like Lockheed Martin, Boeing, and Raytheon but also fueled conflicts in the Middle East, particularly the ongoing war in Yemen, where American-made weapons were used in devastating airstrikes.

Trump's withdrawal from international arms control agreements further escalated the global arms race. His administration abandoned the Intermediate-Range Nuclear Forces (INF) Treaty, a Cold War-era agreement with Russia that had restricted the development of mid-range nuclear weapons. The U.S. also refused to renew the Open Skies Treaty, which allowed mutual surveillance flights to monitor military activities, citing concerns over Russian violations. These moves signaled a return to Cold War-style arms competition, with both the U.S. and Russia accelerating the development of new missile systems. Meanwhile, China ramped up its military expansion in the South China Sea, increasing tensions in the Indo-Pacific region.

Despite Trump's claims that increased defense spending would ensure peace through strength, his administration's policies contributed to heightened global tensions, with rival nations expanding their own military capabilities in response. The defense industry flourished under Trump, but the long-term consequences of his policies included a renewed global arms race, weakened arms control agreements, and increased militarization of new domains like space and cyber warfare. The massive military investments made during Trump's presidency continue to shape U.S. defense strategy, ensuring that competition in military dominance remains a defining feature of international relations in the years ahead.

Privatization of War: Mercenaries and Corporate Influence

The increasing privatization of war has transformed modern conflict, shifting power from national governments to private military companies (PMCs) and defense corporations. Under Donald Trump's presidency, the role of mercenaries and corporate influence in warfare expanded, as the administration sought to reduce traditional military engagements while outsourcing security operations to private contractors. This shift was framed as a cost-effective and politically convenient strategy, allowing the U.S. to maintain a global military presence without the need for large-scale troop deployments. However, the growing reliance on PMCs raised ethical concerns, weakened governmental oversight, and fueled a lucrative war economy where private interests often dictated military strategies.

One of the most notable examples of the privatization of war during Trump's presidency was the increased use of private military contractors (PMCs) in conflict zones like Afghanistan, Iraq, and Syria. While PMCs had been used in past administrations, Trump's approach accelerated their role, particularly after his push to withdraw U.S. troops from key battlegrounds. Companies like Blackwater (later rebranded as Academi), DynCorp, and Triple Canopy played a significant role in providing security, intelligence, and logistical support for U.S. military operations. These private forces often operated in legal gray areas, exempt from the same rules and accountability as traditional military personnel, leading to incidents of human rights violations and civilian casualties.

One of the key figures in Trump's approach to privatized warfare was Erik Prince, the founder of Blackwater and a vocal advocate for replacing conventional military forces with private mercenaries. Prince proposed privatizing the war in Afghanistan, arguing that a corporate-run military operation would be more efficient and cost-effective. While the proposal did not fully materialize, Trump's administration increased its reliance on military contractors in Afghanistan, reducing the number of U.S. troops while keeping a strong presence through PMCs. This strategy allowed the administration to claim it was withdrawing forces while maintaining influence through private military operations.

Beyond combat roles, corporate influence in military policy expanded under Trump, as defense contractors gained unprecedented access to decision-making processes. Trump's administration significantly increased military spending, benefiting companies like Lockheed Martin, Boeing, and Raytheon, which secured billions in government contracts. The revolving door between the Pentagon and private defense firms strengthened corporate influence over military policy, with former executives from defense companies holding key positions in the Trump administration. The result was a military strategy that often prioritized corporate profits over long-term national security objectives, further entrenching the power of the military-industrial complex.

The privatization of war under Trump raised serious concerns about accountability, transparency, and the consequences of delegating military power to profit-driven entities. Private contractors were frequently involved in controversial operations, including drone strikes, intelligence gathering, and special operations, often outside of traditional oversight mechanisms. The increasing use of mercenaries blurred the lines between military operations and corporate interests, allowing conflicts to continue indefinitely as long as they remained profitable for defense firms.

As warfare becomes more privatized, the global landscape of conflict is shifting, with private companies wielding unprecedented influence over military decisions. While the Trump administration's reliance on PMCs and corporate-driven warfare was part of a broader trend, it accelerated the normalization of mercenary forces and strengthened the role of defense corporations in shaping U.S. foreign policy. The long-term implications of this shift remain uncertain, but one thing is clear: the future of war is increasingly dictated not by nations, but by private interests.

The Rise of Extremism and Its Security Threats

The rise of extremism has become one of the most pressing security challenges of the modern era, with radical ideologies fueling violence across political, religious, and nationalist movements. During Donald Trump's presidency, extremist threats evolved, not only from foreign terrorist organizations like ISIS and al-Qaeda but also from domestic radical groups within the United States. The growing influence of far-right nationalist groups, religious fundamentalists, and extremist militias posed significant challenges to national security, leading to heightened political instability, violent attacks, and increased government surveillance efforts. The intersection of radical ideologies, online propaganda, and real-world violence underscored the complexities of modern extremism and its long-term implications for global security.

One of the most significant extremist threats during Trump's tenure was the resurgence of domestic far-right extremism, fueled by nationalist rhetoric, conspiracy theories, and political polarization. Organizations like the Proud Boys, Oath Keepers, and Boogaloo movement gained prominence, often advocating for violence against perceived enemies, including government institutions, racial minorities, and political opponents. The January 6th Capitol riot in 2021 was a stark example of how far-right extremism could escalate into direct attacks on democratic institutions. The riot, carried out by a mix of white nationalist groups, militia members, and conspiracy theorists, demonstrated the growing willingness of extremist movements to use violence as a political tool. The FBI and intelligence agencies increasingly classified domestic extremism as a major security threat, signaling a shift in counterterrorism priorities that had previously been focused primarily on foreign threats.

At the same time, international extremism remained a persistent danger, with ISIS, al-Qaeda, and other jihadist groups continuing to operate despite territorial losses. Although Trump's administration claimed victory over ISIS with the killing of its leader, Abu Bakr al-Baghdadi, the group remained active through decentralized cells and online radicalization efforts. The internet and encrypted messaging apps provided extremist organizations with new ways to recruit followers, spread propaganda, and coordinate attacks. Lone-wolf terrorism, where individuals radicalized online carried out attacks without direct organizational ties, became an increasing concern. This was evident in multiple attacks across Europe and the U.S., where extremists used vehicles, knives, and firearms to target civilians.

The rise of extremism also extended to state-sponsored radicalization, where authoritarian regimes and political leaders used extremist ideologies to strengthen their grip on power. Countries like Russia, Iran, and China were accused of using cyber propaganda to manipulate social unrest in Western nations, amplifying divisive narratives that fueled radical movements. Iran-backed militias in the Middle East carried out attacks against U.S. forces and allies, while Russia allegedly supported far-right groups in Europe to destabilize democratic institutions. These state-sponsored efforts blurred the lines between traditional warfare and ideological extremism, making counterterrorism strategies even more complex.

The growing extremist threats during and after Trump's presidency highlighted the urgent need for comprehensive security measures, including intelligence-sharing, digital counterterrorism efforts, and community-based deradicalization programs. However, the challenge remains in balancing security with civil liberties, as increased government surveillance and counterterrorism laws often spark concerns about privacy and freedom of speech. As extremism continues to evolve, governments worldwide must adapt to the shifting landscape of radical ideologies, ensuring that counterterrorism efforts remain effective while protecting democratic values and social stability.

Chapter 9
Trump's Wars at Home: The Culture and Ideological Divide

Donald Trump's presidency not only reshaped U.S. foreign policy but also deepened domestic cultural and ideological divisions, creating what many described as an internal war within America. His rhetoric and policies amplified partisan conflicts, racial tensions, and debates over national identity, fueling a polarized society where political disagreements turned into existential battles. From immigration policies and racial justice protests to the politicization of science and media, Trump's tenure exposed and exacerbated long-standing fractures in American society. While cultural and ideological divides had existed before his presidency, Trump's leadership style, often marked by combative language and a refusal to seek common ground, escalated these divisions to unprecedented levels.

One of the most defining aspects of Trump's domestic wars was his approach to race relations and social justice movements. His response to incidents like the Charlottesville white nationalist rally in 2017, where he stated there were "very fine people on both sides," and the Black Lives Matter (BLM) protests in 2020 following George Floyd's death, where he called protesters "thugs" and deployed federal forces, underscored his confrontational stance. While his supporters saw him as a defender of law and order, his critics accused him of emboldening white supremacists and stoking racial divisions.

The ideological battle over racial justice, law enforcement, and systemic inequality became one of the most defining and volatile aspects of his presidency, with protests, counter-protests, and violent clashes occurring across the nation.

Beyond racial tensions, Trump also intensified cultural conflicts over gender rights, immigration, and religious freedoms. His administration's policies on border security, the Muslim travel ban, LGBTQ+ rights, and abortion became flashpoints for ideological battles between conservatives and progressives. Trump's Supreme Court appointments further inflamed cultural divisions, as his judicial picks played a crucial role in shaping key rulings on reproductive rights, voting laws, and religious liberties. Meanwhile, his attacks on the media, dismissing critical news coverage as "fake news," eroded trust in journalism, deepening the divide between those who saw the press as a necessary check on power and those who viewed it as an arm of liberal bias. By the time Trump left office, America had become more politically and ideologically fractured than ever, with deep-seated divisions that would continue to shape the nation's political and cultural landscape for years to come.

Domestic Polarization and Its Global Impact

The deep domestic polarization that defined Donald Trump's presidency was not just an internal issue for the United States—it had significant global repercussions. As Trump's rhetoric and policies exacerbated cultural, racial, and ideological divisions within America, these conflicts also influenced U.S. foreign relations, international alliances, and the perception of American leadership on the world stage. The intense political divide, characterized by extreme partisanship, civil unrest, and challenges to democratic norms, weakened the country's ability to project stability and unity abroad.

For both allies and adversaries, the image of a divided America raised questions about its reliability, resilience, and influence in global affairs.

One of the most immediate global consequences of U.S. domestic polarization was the erosion of soft power and diplomatic credibility. Historically, the United States positioned itself as a champion of democracy, human rights, and liberal values, influencing other nations through diplomacy and cultural leadership. However, under Trump, the country saw an increase in political instability, violent protests, and attacks on democratic institutions, most notably the January 6th Capitol riot. These events damaged America's reputation as a stable democracy, giving authoritarian regimes like China, Russia, and Iran the opportunity to discredit the U.S. by portraying it as a failing system. Foreign leaders, who once looked to Washington for guidance, became skeptical of U.S. leadership, uncertain whether the country could maintain a consistent foreign policy when domestic divisions were so intense.

Beyond its diplomatic standing, domestic polarization also impacted U.S. foreign policy and international cooperation. Trump's America First approach, which often dismissed multilateral agreements and longstanding alliances, was rooted in the same nationalist sentiment that fueled domestic divisions. His withdrawal from the Paris Climate Agreement, the Iran Nuclear Deal, and the Trans-Pacific Partnership (TPP) signaled a retreat from global leadership, reinforcing the divide between America and its allies. As domestic conflicts raged over issues like climate change and international trade, foreign governments struggled to negotiate with an administration that often shifted policies based on political pressures at home. This unpredictability made it difficult for allies to rely on U.S. commitments, prompting some to explore alternative economic and strategic partnerships, particularly with China and Russia.

Additionally, the ideological battle over media, truth, and disinformation that fueled polarization in the U.S. had a global impact on the rise of populist and nationalist movements. Trump's tactics—attacking the press, discrediting election results, and promoting conspiracy theories—were replicated by leaders like Jair Bolsonaro in Brazil, Viktor Orbán in Hungary, and Rodrigo Duterte in the Philippines. These leaders used similar strategies to weaken democratic institutions, justify repressive policies, and maintain political power. The spread of digital disinformation campaigns, often amplified by state-sponsored actors in Russia and China, further deepened political divisions not only in the U.S. but also in Europe and Latin America, where populist leaders capitalized on the model set by Trump.

Ultimately, America's domestic polarization reverberated across the global political landscape, influencing everything from diplomatic relations to the strength of democratic institutions worldwide. The inability of the U.S. to resolve its internal conflicts weakened its ability to lead on critical global issues, from trade negotiations to security alliances. As divisions within the country remain deep, the question persists: Can the U.S. reclaim its role as a unifying force in global politics, or will domestic instability continue to diminish its influence on the world stage?

The Role of the Media in Shaping Foreign Policy

The media plays a crucial role in shaping foreign policy by influencing public perception, guiding political discourse, and holding leaders accountable for their international actions. In the age of 24-hour news cycles, digital journalism, and social media, the relationship between media and foreign policy has become more complex than ever. During Donald Trump's presidency, this dynamic was particularly evident, as his administration often clashed with the press while also leveraging media platforms to shape narratives around diplomatic relations, military conflicts, and trade policies. The media's portrayal of international events not only influenced domestic opinions but also affected how foreign leaders and governments engaged with the United States.

One of the most striking examples of media influence on foreign policy was the U.S.-China trade war. The way American and Chinese media outlets framed the economic confrontation played a critical role in shaping public opinion on both sides. In the U.S., conservative media often supported Trump's aggressive stance, portraying China as an economic threat that needed to be countered through tariffs and tougher trade regulations. Meanwhile, mainstream and liberal media outlets highlighted the economic consequences of the trade war, particularly its impact on American farmers, manufacturers, and global supply chains. In China, state-controlled media portrayed the U.S. as an unreliable partner, fueling nationalist sentiment and justifying Beijing's retaliatory economic measures. This media-driven narrative war heightened tensions and made diplomatic resolutions more difficult, as both governments had to respond to public pressure influenced by news coverage.

Another major area where media shaped foreign policy was in U.S. relations with North Korea. Trump's historic meetings with Kim Jong-un were highly publicized, with media outlets closely analyzing every handshake, statement, and negotiation. Trump, who had previously used Twitter to threaten North Korea with military action, later capitalized on the media spectacle surrounding these summits, portraying himself as a diplomatic dealmaker. However, while the media amplified the significance of these meetings, the actual diplomatic progress remained limited, with little concrete change in North Korea's nuclear policies. The intense media coverage created public expectations for peace and denuclearization, but once negotiations stalled, the same media scrutiny contributed to growing skepticism about the effectiveness of Trump's diplomatic approach.

The media also played a critical role in shaping U.S. responses to humanitarian crises and military interventions. Coverage of conflicts in Syria, Yemen, and Venezuela influenced public discourse on whether the U.S. should engage in military action, impose sanctions, or provide humanitarian aid. Graphic images and reports of civilian casualties in Syria led to pressure on the Trump administration to take action against the Assad regime, resulting in U.S. airstrikes in 2017 and 2018. Meanwhile, the media's reporting on the Jamal Khashoggi assassination by Saudi operatives created a diplomatic crisis for the Trump administration, forcing it to navigate the balance between condemning Saudi Arabia's actions and maintaining strong economic and military ties with Riyadh.

The rise of social media and digital disinformation has further complicated the media's role in foreign policy. Platforms like Twitter, Facebook, and YouTube have enabled state actors, including Russia and China, to spread propaganda, manipulate public opinion, and interfere in democratic processes. Trump himself used social media to communicate directly with the public, bypassing traditional media channels and shaping foreign policy narratives through unfiltered statements, threats, and announcements. This direct engagement with digital audiences reshaped diplomatic interactions, sometimes bypassing traditional diplomatic protocols and creating real-time geopolitical tensions.

Ultimately, the media serves as both a watchdog and a battleground for political narratives, influencing how foreign policy is crafted, debated, and executed. While independent journalism can hold leaders accountable and expose foreign policy failures, media polarization and state-controlled propaganda can also deepen misinformation, ideological conflicts, and diplomatic hostilities. In an era where information spreads faster than ever, the role of the media in shaping global affairs remains a powerful force that can either promote transparency and accountability or escalate tensions and misunderstandings on the world stage.

The Rise of Extremism and Its Security Threats

The rise of extremism has become one of the most pressing security challenges of the 21st century, with radical movements fueling violence, political instability, and ideological conflicts across the world. Extremism is no longer confined to a single region or ideology—it spans across political, religious, and nationalist movements, creating a global security crisis that affects democracies, authoritarian regimes, and fragile states alike. During Donald Trump's presidency, the United States and its allies faced evolving threats from both foreign and domestic extremists, including jihadist terrorism, far-right nationalism, and state-sponsored radicalization. The complex nature of modern extremism has made counterterrorism efforts more challenging, as extremist groups exploit digital platforms, misinformation, and societal divisions to spread their influence and incite violence.

One of the most significant sources of extremism remains Islamic jihadist terrorism, with groups like ISIS, al-Qaeda, and their regional affiliates continuing to operate despite military defeats. Trump's administration claimed victory over ISIS with the killing of its leader,

Abu Bakr al-Baghdadi, in 2019, but the group remained active through decentralized cells, online radicalization efforts, and lone-wolf attacks. Islamic extremist organizations have adapted their strategies, shifting from territorial control to cyber recruitment, encrypted communications, and proxy warfare. Attacks in Europe, the Middle East, and Africa demonstrated that jihadist networks still pose a severe security threat, often targeting civilians, government institutions, and Western interests. While the U.S. continued drone strikes and counterterrorism operations against ISIS and al-Qaeda under Trump, the administration's withdrawal from conflict zones like Syria and Afghanistan raised concerns about extremist resurgence in ungoverned spaces.

At the same time, the rise of far-right nationalism and domestic extremism became an increasing concern for U.S. security agencies. Under Trump, white supremacist militias, conspiracy-driven extremists, and anti-government groups gained significant momentum, fueled by political polarization, misinformation, and racial tensions. Organizations such as the Proud Boys, Oath Keepers, and Boogaloo movement promoted violent ideologies, often clashing with law enforcement and left-wing activist groups. The January 6th Capitol riot was a turning point, revealing how far-right extremists could organize large-scale violent events, challenge democratic institutions, and radicalize individuals online. The FBI, DHS, and other intelligence agencies classified far-right extremism as a greater domestic terror threat than foreign jihadist groups, marking a shift in U.S. counterterrorism priorities.

Extremism also extended beyond non-state actors, as authoritarian regimes weaponized radical ideologies to strengthen their grip on power and destabilize rivals. Russia, China, and Iran were accused of using state-sponsored disinformation, cyber propaganda, and proxy groups to manipulate social unrest in Western nations. Russia's interference in the 2016 U.S. election and its support for far-right movements in Europe highlighted how digital extremism could be used to undermine democratic institutions. Meanwhile, Iran-backed militias in the Middle East targeted U.S. military bases, embassies, and allied forces, intensifying regional conflicts. The blurred line between state and non-state extremism made counterterrorism efforts more complex, as governments struggled to address both external threats and radical movements within their own borders.

The rise of extremism in its various forms has forced security agencies, governments, and international coalitions to rethink counterterrorism strategies. While military interventions, intelligence operations, and cybersecurity efforts have helped disrupt extremist networks, the root causes of radicalization—social inequality, political instability, and digital manipulation—remain largely unresolved. Moving forward, nations must develop comprehensive counter-extremism strategies that address both the immediate security threats and the underlying ideological divisions that fuel radical movements. Without a multi-faceted approach, extremism will continue to evolve, posing long-term risks to global peace, democracy, and national security.

Chapter 10
The Future of Global Alliances and Conflicts

As the world transitions into a new era of geopolitical tensions and shifting alliances, the legacy of Donald Trump's presidency continues to influence global relations. His America First policy fundamentally altered U.S. alliances, challenging multilateral institutions, and redefining strategic partnerships. While some of Trump's foreign policies were aimed at strengthening U.S. sovereignty and economic dominance, they also contributed to a more fragmented and competitive international order. The traditional balance of power between the United States, China, Russia, and other emerging global players has shifted, creating uncertainty about the future of global alliances and the potential for renewed conflicts.

The decline of multilateralism, accelerated by Trump's withdrawal from international agreements and skepticism toward organizations like NATO, the United Nations, and the World Trade Organization, has given rise to regional power struggles and economic rivalries. Nations that once relied on strong U.S. leadership have begun forging independent paths, seeking new alliances to safeguard their economic and security interests. China's Belt and Road Initiative (BRI) has positioned Beijing as an alternative global leader, while Russia's military interventions and cyber influence campaigns have intensified its geopolitical footprint. Meanwhile, the

European Union and other Western allies face the challenge of maintaining unity in the absence of clear U.S. direction, leading to complex diplomatic recalibrations.

The future of global alliances will likely be shaped by technological advancements, economic realignments, and emerging security threats. Cyber warfare, artificial intelligence, and space militarization will become key battlegrounds for global influence, requiring new frameworks for cooperation and conflict resolution. Additionally, climate change, resource scarcity, and pandemics will further challenge existing alliances, demanding more adaptive and flexible international partnerships. Whether the world moves toward greater collaboration or deeper divisions will depend on how global powers navigate economic interdependence, military competition, and ideological conflicts in the years ahead.

Can the U.S. Rebuild Global Trust?

The United States has long been a pillar of global leadership, shaping international norms, alliances, and economic policies. However, during Donald Trump's presidency, America's approach to foreign relations took a drastic turn, prioritizing nationalism over multilateralism. The America First policy, marked by withdrawals from key agreements, trade wars, and a general skepticism toward traditional allies, damaged U.S. credibility on the world stage. As a result, many nations began questioning America's reliability as a global partner. Rebuilding trust in U.S. leadership will require a careful balance of diplomacy, strategic alliances, and policy reversals that address the concerns raised during the Trump era.

One of the major obstacles in restoring international confidence is the legacy of withdrawals from multilateral agreements. Trump's decision to exit the Paris Climate Accord, the Iran Nuclear Deal

(JCPOA), and the Trans-Pacific Partnership (TPP) signaled a retreat from global cooperation. These moves not only weakened U.S. influence in shaping international policies but also created power vacuums that were quickly filled by rival nations like China and Russia. While the Biden administration took steps to rejoin some agreements, diplomatic damage had already been done, making allies hesitant to fully trust America's commitments. Moving forward, the U.S. must demonstrate long-term stability in foreign policy, ensuring that international agreements remain resilient despite changes in political leadership.

Another challenge in rebuilding trust is the fractured relationship with traditional allies, particularly in Europe and NATO. Trump's criticisms of NATO, demands for increased defense spending, and trade disputes with the European Union created tensions within the alliance. While NATO survived these strains, U.S. allies were forced to consider greater independence in defense strategies, reducing their reliance on American leadership. To regain credibility, the U.S. must reaffirm its commitments to collective security, strengthen diplomatic ties, and engage in constructive dialogue that reassures allies of its reliability. This will require consistent engagement in global security issues, as well as a willingness to rebuild damaged trade relationships through fair and mutually beneficial agreements.

The rise of China's economic and military power poses another challenge for the U.S. in reestablishing its global leadership. While Trump's administration took an aggressive stance against China through tariffs, trade restrictions, and military posturing in the South China Sea, the approach was often unilateral rather than coordinated with allies. In contrast, China expanded its influence through initiatives like the Belt and Road Initiative (BRI) and diplomatic partnerships with developing nations. To counter China's growing dominance, the U.S. must engage in collaborative economic and security efforts, strengthening partnerships with allies in Asia, Europe, and Latin America to create a more unified approach to global challenges.

Ultimately, rebuilding global trust will require a shift from isolationism to renewed global engagement. The U.S. must recognize that leadership in the modern world is not just about military strength but also about diplomatic credibility, economic cooperation, and technological innovation. By adopting a more consistent and multilateral approach, addressing past missteps, and reaffirming its role as a stable global power, the United States has the potential to restore its influence and rebuild trust with the international community. However, this will require not only policy changes but also a renewed commitment to global stability, transparency, and long-term partnerships.

The Post-Trump World: Recalibrating Diplomacy

In the wake of Donald Trump's presidency, the global diplomatic landscape has undergone significant shifts, requiring the United States to recalibrate its approach to international relations. Trump's America First doctrine redefined U.S. foreign policy by prioritizing unilateral action over multilateral cooperation, often at the expense of long-standing alliances. His administration's withdrawal from international agreements, trade wars, and skepticism toward global institutions left the U.S. in a weakened diplomatic position. As the world moves forward, rebuilding diplomatic relationships and restoring trust will be essential for ensuring stability, economic cooperation, and strategic security in an increasingly multipolar world.

One of the primary challenges in recalibrating diplomacy is repairing strained alliances with traditional partners, particularly in Europe, NATO, and the Asia-Pacific. Trump's frequent criticisms of NATO, his confrontational trade policies with the European Union, and his unpredictable diplomatic strategies created tensions with key allies. The European Union, once heavily aligned with U.S. foreign policy, began exploring more independent defense and trade strategies, while allies like Germany and France questioned America's reliability as a partner. In the Asia-Pacific, Trump's confrontational stance toward China was not always backed by a strong coalition, leading to concerns among regional allies about the U.S.'s long-term commitment to balancing China's influence. Moving forward, the U.S. must reaffirm its commitment to collective security, trade partnerships, and diplomatic consistency, ensuring that allies can once again depend on American leadership in times of geopolitical uncertainty.

Beyond repairing alliances, the post-Trump era presents an opportunity for revitalizing multilateral institutions and diplomatic agreements. Trump's withdrawal from the Paris Climate Accord, the Iran Nuclear Deal (JCPOA), and the Trans-Pacific Partnership (TPP) weakened the U.S.'s ability to shape global policies. These actions not only reduced America's influence in tackling climate change, nuclear proliferation, and economic cooperation but also allowed rival powers like China and Russia to fill the void. While rejoining some agreements is an important first step, diplomacy in the post-Trump world must go further by actively shaping new international frameworks that address modern challenges, such as cybersecurity threats, artificial intelligence governance, and pandemic preparedness. Rather than simply returning to pre-Trump policies, the U.S. must modernize its diplomatic approach to reflect the evolving nature of global power dynamics.

A critical aspect of recalibrating diplomacy will be navigating relations with adversarial nations such as China, Russia, and Iran. Trump's aggressive trade war with China, confrontational stance toward Iran, and ambiguous approach to Russia created significant volatility in global relations. While standing firm against adversaries is necessary, diplomacy requires a balance between strategic deterrence and pragmatic engagement. Future U.S. foreign policy must incorporate clear diplomatic channels with China to manage economic and military tensions, structured negotiations with Iran to prevent nuclear escalation, and a firm yet measured approach to Russia's cyber warfare and geopolitical maneuvers. The challenge is to project strength without alienating potential opportunities for de-escalation and cooperation.

Ultimately, the post-Trump diplomatic landscape requires a strategic recalibration that moves beyond nationalism and unpredictability toward cooperation, stability, and long-term alliances. The world has become more interconnected than ever, and U.S. diplomacy must adapt to this reality by building coalitions, strengthening global governance institutions, and reaffirming its role as a responsible global leader. By restoring credibility, embracing diplomacy over confrontation, and demonstrating consistent engagement, the U.S. can rebuild its international standing and navigate the complexities of a rapidly changing world order.

A New World Order: What Comes Next?

As the world moves beyond the Trump era, geopolitical power structures are shifting, raising critical questions about what comes next for global governance, economic leadership, and international security. The traditional U.S.-led world order, established after World War II, is now facing unprecedented challenges from rising powers, emerging technologies, and shifting alliances. With China's increasing global influence, Russia's strategic maneuvering, and regional coalitions redefining international diplomacy, the post-Trump world is witnessing the early stages of a new global order. Whether this transformation leads to cooperation, competition, or conflict will depend on how nations navigate economic interdependence, military rivalries, and ideological differences.

One of the defining elements of this new world order is the decline of unilateral U.S. dominance. Under Trump, America's withdrawal from global institutions, trade wars, and diplomatic confrontations created a vacuum that China and other emerging powers quickly moved to fill. The Belt and Road Initiative (BRI) has expanded China's economic footprint across Asia, Africa, and Europe, while regional alliances such as the Shanghai Cooperation Organization (SCO) and BRICS continue to grow in influence. Meanwhile, Russia has strengthened its military presence in Eastern Europe, deepened alliances in the Middle East, and engaged in cyber warfare to disrupt Western democracies. These developments signal a move toward a multipolar world, where power is distributed across several key players rather than being concentrated in the hands of the U.S. and its Western allies.

Another major factor shaping the new world order is the role of technology in redefining power structures. Cyber warfare, artificial intelligence, space militarization, and digital surveillance have become central to economic competition and military strategy. Nations are racing to develop advanced AI-driven weaponry, dominate space exploration, and secure control over global digital infrastructure. The rise of state-sponsored hacking, misinformation campaigns, and digital espionage has blurred the lines between war and peace, making traditional security alliances less effective in addressing modern threats. The global balance of power will increasingly be determined by technological superiority, cybersecurity resilience, and digital sovereignty, requiring nations to rethink their defense and economic policies.

Economic realignments are also playing a crucial role in shaping the next phase of global governance. The U.S.-China economic rivalry, exacerbated by Trump's trade wars, has set the stage for a long-term struggle for financial supremacy. As China pushes for de-dollarization and alternative financial systems, global markets are witnessing a shift toward regional trade agreements and digital currencies. The European Union, India, and other middle powers are positioning themselves as independent economic forces, reducing reliance on traditional Western financial institutions. The emergence of regional trading blocs, digital trade platforms, and alternative banking systems could reshape global commerce, challenging the long-standing dominance of Western-led financial structures such as the IMF and World Bank.

Ultimately, the post-Trump world is not just witnessing a shift in leadership but a fundamental transformation of how nations interact and compete. The future will be shaped by new alliances, technological innovations, and economic strategies that challenge the existing global order. Whether this transition leads to greater cooperation or intensifies rivalries remains to be seen, but one thing is clear: the world is entering an era of uncertainty, where the rules of international power are being rewritten. The ability of global leaders to adapt, negotiate, and build strategic partnerships will determine whether the new world order results in stability, conflict, or a completely reimagined system of governance.

Chapter 11
The Climate Crisis and Global Leadership

The climate crisis has emerged as one of the most defining challenges of the 21st century, reshaping global politics, economic strategies, and international alliances. Climate change is no longer just an environmental issue—it is a geopolitical force that influences trade policies, resource conflicts, migration patterns, and global stability. Under Donald Trump's presidency, the U.S. took a dramatic step away from global climate leadership, withdrawing from the Paris Climate Agreement and rolling back numerous environmental regulations. This shift signaled a retreat from cooperative efforts to combat climate change, creating a leadership vacuum that other nations, particularly China and the European Union, sought to fill. As the world faces increasing climate disasters, from extreme weather events to rising sea levels, the role of international leadership in addressing this crisis has become more urgent than ever.

Trump's approach to climate policy was marked by a strong emphasis on fossil fuel expansion and economic deregulation, prioritizing short-term economic growth over long-term sustainability. His administration weakened environmental protections, promoted coal and oil industries, and reduced funding for climate research. By reversing Obama-era policies that aimed to reduce carbon emissions and invest in renewable energy, Trump fundamentally altered the trajectory of U.S. climate action. While these decisions were popular among his political base and fossil fuel industries, they alienated global allies, weakened international climate commitments, and delayed critical actions to combat global warming. The perception that the U.S. was abandoning its responsibilities as a global climate leader led to diplomatic tensions with Europe and increased scrutiny from environmental advocates worldwide.

Despite the U.S. federal government's retreat from climate action, the climate crisis continued to influence global geopolitics, with nations and corporations independently advancing sustainability initiatives. China, the world's largest polluter, seized the opportunity to position itself as a leader in renewable energy investment, launching massive projects in solar, wind, and electric vehicle technology. The European Union, meanwhile, doubled down on its commitment to climate action through initiatives like the European Green Deal, aiming to become carbon-neutral by 2050. Even within the U.S., states like California and New York, along with major corporations, implemented aggressive climate policies despite the federal government's resistance. These decentralized efforts illustrated how the climate movement had become a multi-level issue, driven by not just governments but also private sectors, local authorities, and global institutions.

The post-Trump world must now redefine global leadership on climate issues, addressing the environmental damage done while forging new international commitments. The return of the U.S. to the Paris Climate Agreement under subsequent leadership signaled an attempt to rebuild trust, but the challenge remains in demonstrating consistent, long-term commitment. As climate disasters become more frequent, and resource scarcity leads to geopolitical tensions, the role of international climate cooperation is more critical than ever. The future of climate diplomacy, carbon neutrality goals, and global sustainability efforts will depend on whether world leaders can move beyond political divisions and recognize climate change as a shared global crisis that demands immediate and unified action.

Trump's Withdrawal from the Paris Agreement

Donald Trump's decision to withdraw the United States from the Paris Climate Agreement marked one of the most controversial moments of his presidency and a significant setback for global climate action. The Paris Agreement, adopted in 2015 under President Barack Obama, was a landmark international treaty aimed at limiting global temperature rise to well below 2°C above pre-industrial levels, with an aspirational goal of keeping it below 1.5°C. Nearly 200 countries had committed to reducing greenhouse gas emissions, promoting renewable energy, and transitioning toward a more sustainable global economy. Trump's withdrawal in 2017, citing economic concerns and what he called an unfair disadvantage to the U.S., sent shockwaves through the international community, raising concerns about the future of global climate cooperation.

Trump justified his decision by arguing that the Paris Agreement placed an undue burden on American businesses and workers, particularly in industries such as coal, oil, and manufacturing. He claimed that adhering to the agreement would lead to job losses, increased energy costs, and a decline in U.S. competitiveness compared to nations like China and India, which he argued were given more lenient targets. Trump's administration framed the withdrawal as a move to prioritize economic growth and energy independence, positioning fossil fuel industries as essential to national prosperity. His decision was consistent with his broader

"America First" doctrine, which rejected multilateral agreements in favor of policies that prioritized U.S. interests. However, critics argued that his reasoning misrepresented the structure of the Paris Agreement, which allowed nations to set their own emission reduction targets based on their capabilities and economic conditions.

The withdrawal had significant geopolitical and environmental consequences. The United States, historically the largest cumulative emitter of greenhouse gases, had played a key role in securing the agreement, and its exit undermined global momentum toward climate action. The move also damaged U.S. credibility in international diplomacy, as allies in Europe and beyond saw it as a sign that America was no longer a reliable partner in tackling global challenges. Countries such as France, Germany, and Canada criticized the decision, reaffirming their commitment to the agreement and increasing their climate ambitions. Meanwhile, China seized the opportunity to position itself as a leader in renewable energy and climate diplomacy, expanding its investments in solar, wind, and electric vehicle technologies. Trump's withdrawal thus weakened U.S. influence on global climate policy, allowing other nations to fill the leadership vacuum.

Despite Trump's decision at the federal level, many U.S. states, cities, and corporations pushed back, committing to reducing emissions and supporting clean energy initiatives. Coalitions such as "We Are Still In", composed of governors, mayors, and business leaders, pledged to uphold the principles of the Paris Agreement despite the federal withdrawal. States like California and New York introduced ambitious climate policies, emphasizing that America's commitment to sustainability did not rely solely on the federal government. This response illustrated how climate action had become decentralized, with local and corporate leaders taking a stand even as the White House reversed course.

Ultimately, the U.S. formally withdrew from the Paris Agreement on November 4, 2020, the day after the presidential election, solidifying Trump's stance on climate policy. However, under the Biden administration, the U.S. rejoined the agreement in 2021, signaling an attempt to restore international climate cooperation. While the withdrawal was temporary, it had long-lasting effects on U.S. credibility, climate diplomacy, and global emissions reduction efforts, highlighting the deep political divide in America's approach to climate change. The episode served as a reminder of the fragility of international agreements when political leadership changes, raising concerns about the long-term stability of U.S. climate commitments in an era of growing partisanship.

The Role of Fossil Fuels and Environmental Deregulation

Donald Trump's presidency was marked by a strong emphasis on fossil fuel expansion and widespread environmental deregulation, aligning with his administration's goal of boosting economic growth and energy independence. From the beginning of his tenure, Trump prioritized coal, oil, and natural gas production, rolling back regulations that he argued were stifling the U.S. economy. His administration's aggressive deregulation strategy sought to eliminate environmental restrictions, weaken climate policies, and remove obstacles to fossil fuel development, reversing many of the environmental protections established under previous administrations. While Trump's policies were praised by industry leaders and energy companies, they also faced intense criticism from environmentalists, scientists, and international leaders concerned about the long-term consequences of weakening environmental safeguards.

One of the key pillars of Trump's pro-fossil fuel agenda was the expansion of domestic energy production, including the approval of controversial projects such as the Keystone XL Pipeline and the Dakota Access Pipeline. These projects, which had been stalled under the Obama administration due to environmental concerns, were revived as part of Trump's effort to create jobs and reduce reliance on foreign oil. His administration also opened up federal lands and coastal areas for drilling, lifting restrictions on oil and gas exploration in the Arctic National Wildlife Refuge (ANWR) and offshore waters. By prioritizing fossil fuel extraction, Trump positioned the U.S. as a dominant global energy supplier, arguing that energy independence was critical for economic and national security. However, critics warned that these policies threatened fragile ecosystems, endangered wildlife, and accelerated carbon emissions, exacerbating the climate crisis.

In addition to promoting fossil fuels, Trump's environmental deregulation efforts systematically dismantled key protections designed to combat pollution and climate change. His administration weakened the Clean Power Plan, which had aimed to reduce carbon emissions from power plants, and rolled back fuel efficiency standards for vehicles, allowing higher greenhouse gas emissions from cars and trucks. The Environmental Protection Agency (EPA), under Trump's leadership, was transformed into a business-friendly entity, with regulations on air and water pollution, industrial emissions, and chemical safety significantly loosened. The administration also withdrew Obama-era restrictions on methane emissions, a powerful greenhouse gas that contributes to climate change, allowing oil and gas companies to bypass stricter regulations on leaks and flaring. These rollbacks were framed as efforts to reduce regulatory burdens on businesses, but they also raised concerns about increased air and water pollution, public health risks, and long-term environmental degradation.

Trump's commitment to revitalizing the coal industry became a signature component of his energy policy, despite the fact that coal was already in decline due to market forces. He repeatedly vowed to "bring back coal jobs" by eliminating emissions regulations and easing restrictions on coal mining operations. However, the demand for coal continued to decrease as renewable energy sources and natural gas became more competitive, leading to further closures of coal-fired power plants and job losses in the industry. While Trump's rhetoric on coal was politically powerful in key states like West Virginia and Kentucky, it ultimately did little to revive an industry that was facing structural economic challenges.

The long-term impact of Trump's fossil fuel-driven policies and environmental deregulation remains a subject of debate. Supporters argue that his approach boosted economic growth, created jobs, and strengthened U.S. energy independence, while opponents contend that it undermined global climate efforts, increased pollution, and prioritized short-term gains over long-term sustainability. With the world shifting toward clean energy and climate-conscious policies, Trump's fossil fuel agenda stands as a stark contrast to the growing international movement toward carbon neutrality and environmental responsibility. The deregulation efforts initiated during his presidency may have temporarily benefited fossil fuel industries, but they also raised critical questions about the balance between economic interests and environmental sustainability in the modern era.

Climate Change as a Geopolitical Flashpoint

Climate change has evolved from being primarily an environmental concern to a major geopolitical flashpoint, influencing international relations, economic policies, and global security. As rising temperatures, natural disasters, and resource scarcity reshape the world, nations are increasingly competing for dwindling resources, dealing with climate-induced migration, and navigating the economic transition from fossil fuels to renewable energy. The Trump administration's approach to climate policy—marked by its withdrawal from the Paris Climate Agreement, support for fossil fuel expansion, and rollback of environmental regulations—fueled tensions between the U.S. and its global partners. As climate change intensifies, its role in geopolitical conflicts, economic power shifts, and military strategies is becoming impossible to ignore.

One of the most immediate ways climate change has become a geopolitical flashpoint is through competition over natural resources, particularly water, arable land, and energy sources. Regions such as the Middle East, Sub-Saharan Africa, and South Asia are experiencing severe droughts, leading to food shortages, water crises, and displacement of populations. In places like the Nile River Basin, the Arctic, and the South China Sea, countries are competing for access to critical resources, raising the risk of diplomatic tensions and even military confrontations. The melting of Arctic ice has opened new shipping routes and access to untapped oil and gas reserves, prompting rivalries between nations such as the United States, Russia, Canada, and China. As climate-induced resource conflicts increase, global governance institutions will face mounting challenges in preventing disputes from escalating into full-scale conflicts.

Climate change is also reshaping global migration patterns, creating a humanitarian crisis that has political and security implications. Extreme weather events, rising sea levels, and desertification are forcing millions of people to leave their homes, with the World Bank estimating that climate change could displace over 200 million people by 2050. This climate-driven migration has already contributed to political instability in Europe, Latin America, and South Asia, where climate refugees are putting pressure on governments and fueling nationalist movements. Trump's hardline stance on immigration and efforts to restrict refugee entry did not account for the increasing role of climate change in forced displacement, signaling a lack of long-term strategic planning for dealing with this growing crisis. As climate migration intensifies, it will continue to strain international relations, trigger political unrest, and reshape demographics in many parts of the world.

The global transition from fossil fuels to renewable energy is another key geopolitical flashpoint, as major economies compete to dominate the green energy sector. Countries like China, the European Union, and India are heavily investing in solar, wind, and electric vehicle technology, positioning themselves as leaders in the clean energy revolution. Meanwhile, oil-dependent economies such as Saudi Arabia, Russia, and Venezuela face economic uncertainty as the demand for fossil fuels declines. The U.S., under Trump, prioritized coal, oil, and natural gas, putting American energy policy at odds with the global trend toward sustainability. This divergence led to diplomatic tensions between the U.S. and its allies, particularly in Europe, where climate policy has become a central part of economic planning. The battle over who controls the clean energy future will play a critical role in shaping international power dynamics, trade agreements, and economic alliances in the coming decades.

As climate change continues to exacerbate resource conflicts, migration crises, and economic realignments, its role as a geopolitical flashpoint will only grow. Nations that fail to adapt to the new realities of climate-driven challenges risk falling behind in the emerging global order. Future diplomacy will depend not just on military and economic power but also on climate resilience, sustainable innovation, and international cooperation. The question remains: will global powers choose to work together to address climate change, or will competition for dwindling resources and economic dominance lead to further division and conflict?

Chapter 12
The Pandemic and the Politics of Crisis Management

The COVID-19 pandemic was not just a global health emergency—it became a political and economic crisis that reshaped international relations, exposed governance failures, and tested global cooperation. The pandemic highlighted the strengths and weaknesses of world leaders, governments, and institutions in responding to a fast-moving crisis. Under Donald Trump, the U.S. response to COVID-19 was highly politicized, with decisions often influenced by electoral concerns, ideological divisions, and a broader skepticism toward global health organizations. The handling of the pandemic in the U.S. had far-reaching consequences, not only for American citizens but also for international alliances, trade, and global public health initiatives.

From the onset of the pandemic, Trump's administration downplayed the severity of the virus, dismissing early warnings from health officials and intelligence agencies that COVID-19 had the potential to cause widespread disruption. Trump frequently contradicted scientists and public health experts, portraying lockdown measures and mask mandates as unnecessary or even harmful to economic growth. His administration's early reluctance to acknowledge the gravity of the crisis resulted in delayed containment efforts, overwhelmed healthcare systems, and widespread public confusion. The pandemic quickly became a partisan issue, with

Republican-led states resisting public health measures while Democratic-led states took a more cautious approach. This division extended to vaccine distribution, mask mandates, and school reopenings, further deepening societal polarization and complicating efforts to establish a unified national response.

The economic fallout of the pandemic also became a political battleground. Trump initially resisted large-scale stimulus measures but eventually signed relief packages that included direct payments to Americans, loans to businesses, and support for industries hit hardest by the crisis. However, political infighting in Congress delayed additional aid, leading to increased economic uncertainty. The stock market crash, rising unemployment, and business closures created a recessionary shockwave that forced governments worldwide to reassess economic policies. While Trump repeatedly emphasized economic recovery over public health concerns, critics argued that prioritizing economic reopening without strong public health measures worsened the long-term impact of the crisis. The pandemic revealed deep flaws in the U.S. healthcare system, including disparities in access to medical care, racial and economic inequalities, and the vulnerabilities of a profit-driven healthcare industry.

The international response to COVID-19 was also shaped by politics. Trump frequently clashed with the World Health Organization (WHO), accusing it of being biased toward China and eventually withdrawing U.S. funding from the organization. This decision weakened global efforts to coordinate a pandemic response, as the U.S. had historically played a leading role in global health initiatives. Meanwhile, China used the pandemic as an opportunity to expand its influence, providing medical aid to struggling countries and positioning itself as a global health leader. The lack of international coordination and diplomatic trust contributed to vaccine nationalism, with countries competing for access to doses rather than collaborating on equitable distribution.

The legacy of the pandemic in global politics remains uncertain. While some countries emerged from the crisis with stronger public health infrastructures and renewed commitments to preparedness, others, like the U.S., faced deep societal and political divisions that complicated recovery efforts. The pandemic demonstrated that crisis management is not just about health policies—it is deeply intertwined with leadership, governance, and international cooperation. As future global crises emerge, whether climate disasters, economic collapses, or new pandemics, the lessons from COVID-19 will shape how governments prepare, respond, and navigate the intersection of health, politics, and global security.

The Global Fallout of COVID-19 Policies

The COVID-19 pandemic was not just a public health crisis—it triggered a global economic, social, and political upheaval that reshaped international relations, trade policies, and governance. The policies adopted by different nations to contain the virus varied widely, with some prioritizing strict lockdowns and aggressive public health measures, while others took a more laissez-faire approach. These contrasting strategies led to uneven economic recoveries, intensified geopolitical tensions, and a reevaluation of global institutions. The fallout from these policies continues to be felt across borders, influencing everything from supply chains to vaccine diplomacy and international cooperation.

One of the most immediate and devastating global consequences of COVID-19 policies was the economic recession that resulted from prolonged lockdowns and travel restrictions. Many countries implemented strict stay-at-home orders, business shutdowns, and border closures, leading to widespread job losses, disrupted industries, and financial instability. The global economy contracted by 3.5% in 2020, with some industries—such as tourism, hospitality, and manufacturing—suffering catastrophic declines. Supply chain disruptions further exposed vulnerabilities in global trade, as factory shutdowns in China, shipping delays, and labor shortages caused shortages of essential goods, from medical supplies to semiconductors. Inflation soared in the post-pandemic recovery phase, with high energy costs and supply chain bottlenecks pushing consumer prices up worldwide.

The pandemic also led to growing geopolitical tensions, particularly between the U.S. and China, as accusations over the origins of COVID-19 and responsibility for its spread fueled diplomatic conflicts. Trump repeatedly referred to COVID-19 as the "China virus," escalating tensions between the two superpowers and reinforcing existing trade and political disputes. China, in turn, used the crisis to expand its influence, distributing medical supplies and vaccines to struggling nations through its vaccine diplomacy efforts. Meanwhile, the U.S. and other Western nations were accused of hoarding vaccines, leading to inequalities in global vaccine distribution. This divide underscored the fragility of international solidarity, as wealthier nations secured billions of doses while poorer countries struggled with access. The failure to create a coordinated global response to vaccine distribution highlighted weaknesses in global institutions such as the World Health Organization (WHO) and the United Nations, raising concerns about the world's ability to handle future pandemics.

Social and political instability also emerged as a consequence of pandemic policies, with protests erupting across Europe, the U.S., and

Latin America over lockdown measures, vaccine mandates, and economic hardships. In authoritarian regimes, leaders used the crisis to expand surveillance, suppress dissent, and justify crackdowns on opposition groups, tightening their grip on power. Meanwhile, democratic nations struggled with public distrust, as misinformation, conspiracy theories, and inconsistent messaging from governments led to vaccine skepticism and resistance to public health mandates. The pandemic widened existing societal divisions, exacerbating inequalities in healthcare access, education, and employment, particularly for marginalized communities.

As the world moves beyond the acute phase of the pandemic, its long-term consequences remain uncertain. Nations are reassessing their supply chain dependencies, healthcare preparedness, and economic resilience, while international organizations are pushing for new global health agreements to prevent future pandemics. However, the pandemic exposed deep fractures in global cooperation, economic structures, and governance models, raising critical questions about how nations will rebuild, recover, and prepare for the next global crisis. The fallout from COVID-19 will shape international politics for decades to come, influencing how governments balance public health, economic stability, and national security in an increasingly interconnected world.

Vaccine Diplomacy and International Cooperation

Vaccine diplomacy emerged as a critical factor in global relations during the COVID-19 pandemic, as countries leveraged vaccine production and distribution to expand their influence and secure strategic partnerships. The rapid development of vaccines was a scientific achievement, but their distribution became a political tool, with wealthier nations and major powers using vaccines as leverage in international negotiations. While global cooperation played a role in vaccine access, disparities between wealthy and developing nations revealed deep flaws in international health systems. Countries such as China, Russia, and the United States took different approaches to vaccine diplomacy, each seeking to enhance their geopolitical standing through medical aid.

China positioned itself as a leader in vaccine diplomacy by supplying doses to developing nations, particularly in Africa, Latin America, and Southeast Asia. The Chinese government actively promoted its Sinopharm and Sinovac vaccines as alternatives to Western options, sending millions of doses to countries struggling with vaccine shortages. In exchange, China strengthened its economic and political ties with recipient nations, many of which were part of its Belt and Road Initiative. Russia followed a similar strategy, using its Sputnik V vaccine to forge stronger relationships in Latin America, Eastern Europe, and the Middle East. By supplying vaccines to nations with limited access to Western pharmaceutical companies, Russia aimed to expand its influence in regions where it had previously struggled to compete with the United States and European Union. However, both China and Russia faced skepticism over the efficacy and transparency of their vaccines, with concerns about data reliability leading some countries to seek alternative suppliers.

The United States and European nations, on the other hand, initially focused on domestic vaccination efforts before engaging in international vaccine diplomacy. The early months of the pandemic saw Western countries securing vast supplies of Pfizer, Moderna, and AstraZeneca vaccines, while developing nations struggled to access doses. This vaccine hoarding led to criticism that the wealthiest countries were prioritizing their populations at the expense of global equity. Eventually, as Western nations reached high vaccination rates, the U.S. and its allies shifted their focus to global distribution through initiatives like COVAX, a program designed to ensure fair vaccine access worldwide. The Biden administration ramped up donations, pledging millions of doses to Africa, Asia, and Latin America, while the European Union implemented similar initiatives to supply vaccines to lower-income nations. These efforts, while significant, came late in the pandemic, after China and Russia had already used vaccine diplomacy to build influence.

The disparities in vaccine access during COVID-19 highlighted broader issues in global health governance. While vaccine diplomacy provided an opportunity for countries to extend goodwill and strengthen alliances, it also exposed inequalities in distribution, as wealthier nations controlled much of the supply. Many developing countries faced logistical challenges, lacking the infrastructure needed to store and distribute vaccines effectively. The pandemic underscored the need for a more coordinated international approach to future health crises, including agreements on equitable vaccine distribution, investment in global healthcare infrastructure, and improved international cooperation. Moving forward, the lessons from COVID-19 vaccine diplomacy will shape how nations handle future pandemics, determining whether medical aid will be used as a tool for political gain or as a means for genuine global solidarity.

The Reshaping of Global Public Health Infrastructure

The COVID-19 pandemic forced the world to confront weaknesses in global public health infrastructure, exposing vulnerabilities in healthcare systems, supply chains, and pandemic preparedness. The crisis led to a reassessment of how nations approach public health, with governments, international organizations, and private sectors scrambling to address gaps in healthcare capacity and disease prevention. Countries that had previously underfunded public health were forced to invest heavily in medical research, vaccine development, and healthcare accessibility. Meanwhile, global institutions such as the World Health Organization (WHO) faced both increased reliance and sharp criticism, as their ability to coordinate a worldwide response was tested in unprecedented ways. The reshaping of global public health infrastructure is now underway, with nations and organizations seeking to build resilience against future pandemics while navigating the geopolitical and economic challenges that accompany such reforms.

One of the most immediate responses to the pandemic was the rapid mobilization of resources to expand healthcare infrastructure. Hospitals around the world struggled with surging patient numbers, revealing shortages of ventilators, intensive care unit beds, and frontline medical workers. Governments rushed to set up emergency hospitals, secure medical supplies, and strengthen healthcare systems that were stretched beyond their limits. The pandemic also accelerated investment in medical research and biotechnology, leading to unprecedented collaboration between pharmaceutical companies, governments, and research institutions. The development of mRNA vaccines by companies such as Pfizer-BioNTech and Moderna demonstrated how rapidly medical science could adapt when given the necessary funding and global cooperation. However, disparities in healthcare access became apparent as wealthier nations dominated vaccine procurement while lower-income countries faced long delays, further underscoring the need for a more equitable global health strategy.

Beyond emergency responses, the pandemic reshaped how governments plan for future health crises. Many nations restructured their public health agencies, improving early warning systems, pandemic preparedness protocols, and supply chain resilience. Countries that had experienced past pandemics, such as South Korea and Taiwan, used their experience with previous outbreaks to implement strict public health measures, including digital contact tracing and mass testing. In contrast, Western nations, including the United States and several European countries, faced criticism for their delayed responses, inconsistent messaging, and politicization of public health measures. The need for stronger global coordination became evident as fragmented national policies led to mixed results, with some nations struggling to contain the virus while others successfully implemented aggressive containment strategies.

The role of international organizations in managing public health infrastructure also came under scrutiny. The WHO was at the center of global pandemic response efforts, yet its authority and credibility were challenged, particularly by nations such as the United States under Donald Trump, who accused it of failing to hold China accountable for the virus's early spread. The pandemic revealed the limits of global health governance, as nations often prioritized national interests over coordinated international efforts. This has led to discussions about reforming global health institutions to ensure greater transparency, funding, and accountability in future crises.

As nations emerge from the pandemic, the reshaping of global public health infrastructure is an ongoing process. Countries are investing in stronger surveillance systems, improving emergency medical supply chains, and reassessing the role of international cooperation in public health. The pandemic underscored that health security is not just a national issue but a global one, requiring sustained commitment from governments, organizations, and private sectors to build a resilient and equitable healthcare system for the future. The lessons learned from COVID-19 will shape how the world responds to future health threats, determining whether preparedness efforts will prevent another global catastrophe or whether history will repeat itself.

Chapter 13
The Role of Technology in Shaping Geopolitics

In the modern world, technology has become one of the most significant drivers of geopolitical power, transforming how nations compete, cooperate, and exert influence on the global stage. From artificial intelligence and cybersecurity to digital surveillance and space exploration, technological advancements are reshaping international relations, military strategy, and economic dominance. As the world moves deeper into the digital age, countries are no longer just competing for land, natural resources, or military superiority—they are fighting for control over data, infrastructure, and emerging technologies. The battle for technological supremacy is no longer just between governments but also between corporations, intelligence agencies, and cyber actors operating across borders.

The competition between the United States and China in the realm of technology has become one of the defining aspects of 21st-century geopolitics. Both nations see artificial intelligence (AI), quantum computing, and 5G networks as key to their national security and economic strength. The U.S. has historically led the world in innovation, with Silicon Valley housing some of the most influential tech companies, including Google, Apple, and Microsoft. However, China's rapid advancements in semiconductor manufacturing, AI research, and telecommunications, led by companies like Huawei, Tencent, and Alibaba, have positioned it as a formidable competitor. This tech rivalry has resulted in trade restrictions, sanctions, and government interventions, with the U.S. imposing bans on Chinese firms over security concerns and China accelerating its push for technological self-reliance. This ongoing battle for digital dominance is reshaping alliances, as countries are forced to align themselves with either the Western-led tech ecosystem or the China-led digital infrastructure.

Cybersecurity has also emerged as a major geopolitical battleground, as cyber warfare and hacking campaigns have become tools for espionage, sabotage, and political disruption. Nations like Russia, China, North Korea, and Iran have been accused of conducting cyberattacks on Western institutions, targeting critical infrastructure, financial systems, and democratic processes. The 2016 U.S. election saw foreign interference through social media manipulation, email hacking, and disinformation campaigns, highlighting the growing threat of digital warfare in political decision-making. In response, governments have invested heavily in cyber defense capabilities, creating specialized military divisions for cybersecurity and expanding intelligence-sharing networks with allies. The ability to defend against cyber threats and launch countermeasures has become just as crucial as conventional military strength in modern geopolitical strategy.

Beyond cyberspace, space technology and artificial intelligence are also playing a critical role in shaping international power dynamics. The militarization of space, with countries developing anti-satellite weapons, satellite surveillance, and space-based communication networks, has introduced a new arena for strategic competition. AI-driven technologies, from autonomous drones and facial recognition to algorithmic warfare and automated decision-making, are revolutionizing military capabilities and intelligence operations. The ethical implications of AI in warfare, surveillance, and governance have sparked debates on how to balance national security with civil liberties and human rights. Countries that can harness AI, robotics, and biotechnology will gain a significant strategic advantage in the coming decades.

As technology continues to evolve at an unprecedented pace, nations that can innovate, regulate, and secure their digital and technological infrastructure will shape the future of global power. However, the absence of global regulations, ethical concerns, and the risk of technological misuse present major challenges. Whether technology becomes a force for cooperation or conflict will depend on how world leaders navigate this new era of digital geopolitics, ensuring that technological advancements serve humanity rather than becoming tools of division and authoritarian control.

Big Tech, Censorship, and Global Influence

The rise of Big Tech has profoundly reshaped global geopolitics, shifting power from traditional government institutions to private technology corporations that control vast amounts of data, communication platforms, and digital infrastructure. Companies like Google, Facebook (Meta), Amazon, Apple, Microsoft, and Twitter (now X) have expanded their influence beyond national borders, making them key players in global affairs. These firms have amassed unprecedented power over information, commerce, and communication, raising concerns about censorship, political manipulation, national security, and digital sovereignty. As governments attempt to regulate these platforms, tensions have emerged over how much control Big Tech should have over free speech, content moderation, and political discourse, and whether their decisions serve corporate interests or align with democratic values.

One of the most controversial aspects of Big Tech's influence is its role in content moderation and censorship. Social media platforms have become the primary means through which billions of people consume news, express opinions, and engage in political activism. However, the ability of private companies to control the flow of information, deplatform individuals, and remove content has sparked intense debate. During Donald Trump's presidency, the issue of censorship came to the forefront when major platforms suspended Trump's accounts following the January 6th Capitol riot, citing concerns over incitement to violence. While some praised the move as necessary to prevent harm, others saw it as an overreach of corporate power, arguing that private companies should not have the authority to silence elected officials. This raised fundamental questions about who decides what speech is acceptable in the digital age and whether tech companies are acting as neutral platforms or gatekeepers of political discourse.

Beyond the U.S., Big Tech's role in global censorship and information control has had wide-reaching consequences. In authoritarian regimes, governments have used pressure, regulatory policies, and cyber laws to force tech companies to comply with censorship demands. China's Great Firewall is the most extreme example, where companies like Google and Facebook are blocked, and domestic platforms such as WeChat and Weibo operate under strict state surveillance. However, even in countries with democratic traditions, governments have pushed for greater oversight of online content, citing concerns over misinformation, hate speech, and national security threats. The European Union has imposed strict regulations on digital content, while India and Russia have forced platforms to comply with government requests to remove politically sensitive material. This global trend toward digital control raises concerns about whether tech companies are protecting freedom of speech or enabling state censorship.

The growing influence of Big Tech in shaping elections, influencing public opinion, and manipulating algorithms has also fueled debates about corporate responsibility. Algorithmic bias, targeted advertising, and political misinformation have been major concerns, as tech companies have been accused of amplifying divisive content to maximize engagement and profits. The role of social media in events such as the Arab Spring, Brexit, and the U.S. elections has shown that digital platforms can be used both for democratic activism and for spreading disinformation. Meanwhile, governments have struggled to develop regulations that balance protecting online freedoms with preventing harmful content.

As the battle over censorship, free speech, and digital governance continues, Big Tech's role in global politics will remain under intense scrutiny. The power of private corporations to shape political narratives, silence voices, and influence global policies has led to growing calls for greater accountability, transparency, and regulatory oversight. Whether governments can successfully rein in the power of Big Tech without compromising internet freedom and innovation will be one of the defining challenges of the digital age.

The Rise of Surveillance States and Digital Authoritarianism

The rapid advancement of digital technology has enabled governments around the world to expand their surveillance capabilities, leading to the rise of surveillance states and digital authoritarianism. With access to facial recognition, artificial intelligence (AI), big data analytics, and cyber monitoring tools, governments can now track individuals, suppress dissent, and manipulate public opinion with unprecedented precision. While some nations justify these measures as necessary for national security and crime prevention, critics argue that mass surveillance erodes civil liberties, undermines democracy, and enables authoritarian control. The increasing use of digital surveillance by both authoritarian regimes and democratic governments raises urgent questions about privacy, human rights, and the balance between security and freedom in the digital age.

China has become the most prominent example of a fully developed surveillance state, using technology to exert near-total control over its population. The Chinese government has deployed millions of AI-powered surveillance cameras, biometric tracking systems, and digital monitoring tools to track citizens in real time. Through its Social Credit System, individuals are scored based on their online activities, financial transactions, and even personal behavior, influencing their access to jobs, loans, and public services. Additionally, China has censored the internet through the Great Firewall, blocking foreign websites and controlling domestic platforms like WeChat and Weibo to ensure that online discourse aligns with state-approved narratives. These surveillance mechanisms allow the Chinese Communist Party to suppress dissent, monitor ethnic minorities such as the Uyghurs in Xinjiang, and eliminate political opposition. The success of China's surveillance model has made it a blueprint for other authoritarian regimes, which see digital authoritarianism as a way to maintain control while avoiding overt repression.

Russia, Iran, and North Korea have also adopted digital surveillance to tighten their grip on power. Russia has implemented strict internet laws, requiring tech companies to store data on local servers and comply with government censorship. The Kremlin has used cyber surveillance to track opposition activists, manipulate online discourse, and spread disinformation both domestically and internationally. Iran, facing domestic protests and political opposition, has developed its own national internet infrastructure, allowing the government to control access to foreign websites and cut off online communications during protests. North Korea, one of the most closed-off nations in the world, has built a tightly controlled digital ecosystem that allows only state-approved content, effectively isolating its citizens from global information networks. These countries demonstrate how digital tools can be weaponized to maintain political power, suppress dissent, and manipulate public perception.

Even in democratic nations, concerns over mass surveillance and digital control are growing. Governments in the United States, Europe, and India have expanded their use of facial recognition, AI surveillance, and data tracking under the justification of counterterrorism, national security, and law enforcement. The Edward Snowden revelations exposed the extent of government-led mass surveillance by the NSA, sparking global debates about privacy rights and state overreach. In the European Union, new regulations on AI and data privacy attempt to balance security with civil liberties, but concerns remain about how much power governments should have over digital infrastructure.

The rise of surveillance states and digital authoritarianism poses a direct threat to democracy, freedom of expression, and human rights. As governments continue to expand their digital monitoring capabilities, the challenge for the international community will be to establish legal frameworks and global norms that protect privacy while ensuring security. Without strong oversight and accountability, the risk of a world where digital surveillance becomes the default mechanism of governance is becoming increasingly real.

The Battle for Technological Supremacy

The race for technological supremacy has become one of the defining conflicts of the 21st century, shaping economic power, military strength, and global influence. Nations are no longer just competing in traditional areas of industry and commerce but are now locked in a high-stakes battle for dominance in artificial intelligence (AI), quantum computing, cybersecurity, space technology, and 5G networks. This battle is largely centered around the United States and China, two superpowers vying for control over the technologies that will define the future. Their competition has fueled trade wars, intelligence operations, and economic policies aimed at securing technological independence. The outcome of this struggle will determine which nation leads the world in innovation and dictates the rules of the digital age.

The competition between the U.S. and China is most evident in semiconductors, AI, and telecommunications infrastructure. Semiconductors, the building blocks of modern technology, are at the heart of this conflict. The U.S. has historically dominated the semiconductor industry, with companies like Intel, NVIDIA, and Qualcomm leading innovation. However, China has aggressively invested in domestic chip production and AI research, with companies like Huawei and SMIC (Semiconductor Manufacturing International Corporation) aiming to reduce reliance on Western technology. The U.S. has imposed export restrictions on advanced chip technology to slow China's progress, while China has responded by increasing funding for its own semiconductor industry. This technological decoupling is pushing both nations toward self-sufficiency, raising concerns about the fragmentation of the global tech supply chain.

Artificial intelligence is another critical battleground in the fight for technological supremacy. The U.S. has been the leader in AI research, with tech giants like Google, Microsoft, and OpenAI developing cutting-edge machine learning models. However, China is catching up rapidly, integrating AI into military applications, surveillance systems, and smart cities. The Chinese government has set ambitious goals to become the world leader in AI by 2030, funding research in areas like facial recognition, autonomous weapons, and AI-powered cyber warfare. The military implications of AI dominance are significant, as it could determine which country gains an edge in autonomous warfare, cyber espionage, and predictive intelligence.

The global rollout of 5G networks has also become a major flashpoint in the tech war. Huawei, China's telecommunications giant, has led the charge in developing 5G infrastructure, offering high-speed connectivity to nations around the world. The U.S., however, has aggressively pushed back against Huawei, citing national security concerns and urging allies to ban the company from their 5G networks. The fear is that China could use Huawei's technology for cyber espionage and intelligence gathering, leading many Western nations to develop alternative infrastructure with companies like Ericsson and Nokia. The battle over 5G is not just about faster internet—it is about who controls the backbone of future digital economies, cybersecurity systems, and data flows.

The battle for technological supremacy will not only shape economic policies and trade alliances but also determine the future of military capabilities, surveillance networks, and global governance. Nations that control these emerging technologies will set the rules for cybersecurity, data privacy, and international AI ethics. As the rivalry between the U.S. and China intensifies, the world faces a crucial question: Will this competition drive innovation and progress, or will it lead to digital fragmentation, cyber warfare, and a new Cold War over technology?

Chapter 14
U.S. Influence in Latin America: A Declining Power?

For much of the 20th and early 21st centuries, the United States maintained dominant influence over Latin America, shaping the region's political, economic, and security landscape through a combination of diplomacy, economic policies, military interventions, and trade agreements. However, in recent years, U.S. influence in the region has faced significant challenges, with China, Russia, and regional powers stepping in to fill the vacuum left by Washington's shifting priorities. The Trump administration's approach to Latin America was characterized by hardline immigration policies, economic sanctions, and a transactional diplomatic style that alienated some traditional allies while failing to counter the rising influence of external players. As a result, Latin America has become a contested geopolitical battleground, where the question remains: Is U.S. dominance in the region declining irreversibly?

One of the primary factors contributing to the erosion of U.S. influence in Latin America has been Washington's inconsistent engagement with the region. While past administrations pursued diplomatic ties, economic investments, and regional cooperation initiatives, the Trump administration often prioritized border security and immigration concerns over strategic partnerships. The controversial zero-tolerance immigration policy, which led to family separations at the U.S.-Mexico border, strained relations with key allies in Central and South America. Additionally, Trump's threats to cut foreign aid to countries such as El Salvador, Honduras, and Guatemala—nations already struggling with economic hardship and violence—further weakened U.S. credibility. These policies contributed to a growing perception that the United States was more interested in punishing its neighbors than fostering long-term regional stability.

Meanwhile, China has significantly expanded its economic footprint in Latin America, offering large-scale infrastructure investments, loans, and trade agreements through its Belt and Road Initiative (BRI). China is now the largest trading partner for several South American nations, including Brazil, Chile, and Peru, outpacing the U.S. in key industries such as mining, agriculture, and energy. This shift has been driven by China's demand for natural resources, as well as its willingness to provide low-interest loans and funding for infrastructure projects with fewer political conditions than those imposed by U.S.-backed institutions like the International Monetary Fund (IMF). Many Latin American leaders, frustrated with U.S. austerity measures and political interference, have welcomed China's economic support as an alternative to traditional Western influence.

At the same time, Russia has sought to expand its strategic presence in Latin America, particularly through military alliances and energy deals. Moscow has strengthened ties with Venezuela, Cuba, and Nicaragua, offering military aid, intelligence cooperation, and diplomatic support. In Venezuela, Russia played a critical role in propping up Nicolás Maduro's regime, helping Caracas withstand U.S. sanctions and diplomatic pressure. These alliances underscore a broader shift in Latin America's geopolitical landscape, where nations are increasingly willing to diversify their international partnerships rather than rely solely on Washington's backing.

As Latin America becomes a more multipolar region, the U.S. faces an uphill battle in reasserting its influence. If Washington fails to adapt its strategy—focusing on economic engagement, fair trade, and diplomatic partnerships rather than relying on coercion—its once-dominant role in the region may continue to decline. The question remains: Can the U.S. reclaim its leadership in Latin America, or will China, Russia, and regional powers reshape the future of the hemisphere?

Trade, Sanctions, and Economic Pressure in the Region

U.S. economic policy in Latin America has long been defined by a mix of trade agreements, sanctions, and financial aid, aimed at securing Washington's influence and shaping the region's economic and political landscape. However, in recent years, this influence has been increasingly challenged by external players, particularly China, Russia, and regional economic shifts. The Trump administration's approach to Latin America focused on economic pressure through sanctions and renegotiated trade deals, but these strategies often alienated traditional allies and pushed some countries closer to alternative economic partners. As the balance of power shifts, Latin America is becoming a more contested space for economic influence, with new trade alliances and economic pressures redefining its relationship with the United States.

One of the most significant economic shifts in Latin America has been the rise of China as a dominant trading partner, challenging Washington's long-standing economic control over the region. Over the past two decades, China has dramatically increased its trade, investment, and infrastructure projects in Latin America, surpassing the U.S. as the largest trading partner for Brazil, Chile, Peru, and Argentina. Through its Belt and Road Initiative (BRI), China has provided billions of dollars in loans and infrastructure development, financing projects in energy, mining, transportation, and telecommunications. Unlike the United States, which often attaches political conditions to its financial aid, China's investments come with fewer restrictions, making them more attractive to Latin American governments seeking economic growth. This shift has weakened Washington's leverage in the region, as more countries turn to Beijing for economic partnerships and financial stability.

The Trump administration's economic policies toward Latin America were largely defined by sanctions and trade renegotiations, particularly in dealings with Mexico, Venezuela, and Cuba. One of Trump's key economic moves was renegotiating NAFTA, resulting in the United States-Mexico-Canada Agreement (USMCA), which aimed to secure more favorable terms for American businesses while tightening labor and environmental regulations. While this deal maintained strong trade ties between the U.S. and Mexico, Trump's threats to impose tariffs on Mexican exports in response to immigration concerns created tensions between the two countries. Additionally, sanctions on Venezuela and Cuba were intensified under Trump, targeting the regimes of Nicolás Maduro and Miguel Díaz-Canel with severe economic restrictions. While these sanctions were intended to cripple authoritarian governments and force political change, they often had devastating effects on ordinary citizens, exacerbating economic crises and increasing migration flows to the U.S.

Despite Washington's continued use of economic pressure, Latin American nations are increasingly seeking to diversify their trade partnerships and reduce dependence on the U.S. market. The creation of regional trade blocs, such as the Pacific Alliance and Mercosur, has strengthened intra-Latin American trade, allowing nations to form independent economic strategies that are less reliant on Washington's policies. Additionally, countries like Argentina and Brazil have deepened ties with the European Union, signing trade agreements that challenge America's economic primacy in the region.

As Latin America's economy becomes more interconnected with global markets, the effectiveness of U.S. sanctions and economic pressure is being called into question. If Washington wants to maintain influence, it must shift from punitive economic strategies to cooperative engagement, offering meaningful trade agreements, investment opportunities, and diplomatic partnerships that can compete with China's expanding presence. Without this adjustment, the U.S. risks further diminishing its economic dominance in a region that has historically been within its sphere of influence.

The Rise of Left-Wing Governments and U.S. Policy Shifts

In recent years, Latin America has experienced a resurgence of left-wing governments, challenging U.S. influence in the region and reshaping diplomatic and economic policies. Historically, the United States has maintained close ties with Latin America, often supporting right-leaning or centrist governments that align with its economic and strategic interests. However, the shift towards progressive, socialist, and populist leaders in countries like Mexico, Argentina, Chile, Colombia, and Brazil has led to new challenges for Washington, requiring a recalibration of U.S. policy in the region. The return of left-wing leadership, often driven by economic inequality, social movements, and dissatisfaction with past neoliberal policies, has led to increasing friction between the U.S. and Latin American nations, particularly on issues such as trade, sanctions, foreign aid, and diplomatic relations.

One of the most significant developments in this political shift was the election of Andrés Manuel López Obrador (AMLO) in Mexico in 2018. As a leftist populist, AMLO's leadership has emphasized social programs, economic nationalism, and reducing Mexico's dependence on U.S. policies. While trade relations between the U.S. and Mexico remained strong under the United States-Mexico-Canada Agreement (USMCA), AMLO often took a non-confrontational but independent approach in dealing with the Trump administration, particularly on immigration, energy policy, and security cooperation. His resistance to U.S. pressure on issues like asylum policies and drug enforcement signaled a shift in Mexico's willingness to comply with Washington's demands without negotiation. This represents a broader trend across Latin America, where left-wing leaders are increasingly prioritizing regional autonomy over alignment with U.S. interests.

Brazil, the largest economy in Latin America, has also witnessed a major political shift with the return of Luiz Inácio Lula da Silva in 2023, replacing the right-wing government of Jair Bolsonaro. Lula's presidency marks a return to progressive economic policies, stronger ties with regional partners, and a more independent foreign policy stance. Unlike Bolsonaro, who cultivated close ties with Trump and aligned with Washington's anti-China rhetoric, Lula has strengthened Brazil's relationship with China and the European Union, signaling a shift away from U.S. economic dominance. Additionally, his focus on climate change and the Amazon rainforest has led to tensions with U.S. policymakers, who have historically pressured Brazil on environmental policies while maintaining economic interests in the region's natural resources.

The resurgence of leftist governments in Chile, Colombia, Argentina, and Peru further underscores this regional transformation. Leaders such as Gabriel Boric in Chile and Gustavo Petro in Colombia have prioritized social justice, wealth redistribution, and indigenous rights, policies that sometimes clash with Washington's economic and investment priorities. Many of these leaders have also been vocal critics of U.S. interventions in Latin America, opposing sanctions on Venezuela and Cuba while advocating for greater regional unity through organizations like CELAC (Community of Latin American and Caribbean States). This rejection of U.S.-backed neoliberal policies has fueled debates over whether Washington should continue using sanctions and diplomatic pressure or adapt its strategy to engage more constructively with the region's shifting political landscape.

As Latin America moves toward greater regional integration and reduced U.S. dependence, Washington faces a diplomatic crossroads. To maintain influence, the U.S. must adopt a more flexible and cooperative approach, recognizing the legitimacy of leftist governments rather than resorting to economic pressure or political isolation. The era of unilateral U.S. dominance in Latin America is fading, and its future role in the region will depend on whether it embraces diplomatic pragmatism or continues to resist the region's evolving political reality.

Conclusion

The world has undergone a profound transformation over the past decade, with global conflicts, shifting alliances, economic upheavals, and technological advancements shaping the course of international relations. Donald Trump's presidency played a pivotal role in accelerating these changes, redefining the balance of power, trade policies, diplomatic engagements, and military strategies. As the United States recalibrates its global position in the post-Trump era, it faces unprecedented challenges and new geopolitical realities that will determine whether it can maintain its leadership role or cede influence to emerging superpowers like China and Russia.

Trump's America First policy sought to disrupt the established international order, prioritizing nationalist interests over multilateral agreements and reshaping the United States' relationships with key allies and adversaries. His administration's withdrawal from global institutions, trade agreements, and climate initiatives weakened Washington's diplomatic standing and allowed competing powers to step into the void. China, for example, used this period to expand its economic footprint in Latin America, Africa, and Asia, while Russia strengthened its military and cyber influence in Eastern Europe, the Middle East, and beyond. The erosion of multilateralism, coupled with domestic polarization and economic nationalism, created an environment where alliances were tested, conflicts intensified, and new power structures emerged.

One of the most enduring effects of Trump's foreign policy was the rise of nationalist and populist movements around the world. His rhetoric emboldened strongmen leaders, from Jair Bolsonaro in Brazil to Viktor Orbán in Hungary, who adopted similar tactics of attacking democratic institutions, suppressing media freedoms, and challenging international norms. This shift toward authoritarianism and illiberal democracy has had lasting consequences, weakening democratic institutions and increasing political instability in regions that were previously committed to liberal governance. The question remains whether this trend will continue or whether a renewed emphasis on democracy and international cooperation can reverse its momentum.

The geopolitical competition between the U.S. and China has become the defining conflict of the 21st century, extending beyond trade wars into areas like military posturing, technological dominance, and ideological influence. The battle for control over semiconductors, artificial intelligence, 5G networks, and cybersecurity is shaping the future of global power, with both nations racing to outpace one another in these critical areas. While the Trump administration sought to counter China through tariffs, sanctions, and diplomatic isolation, Beijing responded with economic expansion, strategic partnerships, and technological investments that have solidified its position as a global superpower. The U.S. now faces a complex and evolving challenge: How can it counterbalance China's rise without escalating into direct military confrontation?

Russia's renewed aggression and cyber influence have also added to global instability. While Trump often took a controversial stance on U.S.-Russia relations, including questionable admiration for Vladimir Putin, Russia remained an active adversary, using cyber warfare, election interference, and military interventions to challenge Western democracies. The Ukraine crisis and NATO's response highlighted the need for the U.S. and its allies to strengthen their collective security measures while addressing Russia's strategic ambitions. The effectiveness of these efforts will determine whether NATO and the Western alliance can maintain their strength in an era of rising authoritarianism.

Beyond traditional geopolitical conflicts, climate change, cyber warfare, and global health crises have emerged as new battlegrounds for international competition and cooperation. The COVID-19 pandemic exposed weaknesses in global health infrastructure, revealing gaps in pandemic preparedness, vaccine distribution, and international cooperation. The United States, under Trump, struggled to manage its response effectively, leading to economic fallout, social unrest, and diminished global credibility. Meanwhile, climate change has continued to destabilize regions, fuel resource conflicts, and reshape migration patterns, forcing governments to reconsider their commitments to environmental policies and sustainable development. As these non-traditional security threats grow, the need for global coordination and strategic resilience has never been greater.

The role of Big Tech and digital authoritarianism has further complicated global power dynamics, as governments increasingly rely on surveillance, artificial intelligence, and cyber capabilities to assert control. While the U.S. and its allies advocate for open digital societies and data privacy, authoritarian regimes have leveraged technology to suppress dissent, manipulate information, and expand their geopolitical influence. The debate over censorship, free speech, and the ethical use of technology will shape the next era of geopolitical competition, determining whether technology serves as a tool for democracy or a weapon for oppression.

Latin America has also witnessed significant shifts in political and economic influence, with the U.S. struggling to maintain its historic dominance in the region. The rise of left-wing governments, increased Chinese economic investment, and Russia's military partnerships have signaled a shift away from U.S. hegemony toward a more multipolar regional order. If Washington fails to engage with Latin America in a meaningful and cooperative way, it risks losing influence to rival nations that offer alternative economic models and diplomatic strategies.

Looking ahead, the post-Trump world presents both risks and opportunities. The United States can choose to rebuild its alliances, reassert its leadership in multilateral institutions, and invest in emerging technologies and sustainable energy to regain its global influence. However, if it continues down the path of isolationism, economic protectionism, and internal political division, its ability to shape the world order will diminish. The balance of power is shifting, and how the U.S. responds to these changes will define its role in global affairs for decades to come.

Ultimately, the future of global stability depends on whether nations can navigate these evolving conflicts through diplomacy, cooperation, and technological innovation, or whether rivalry and fragmentation will lead to greater instability and confrontation. The coming years will test the ability of world leaders to manage geopolitical tensions, adapt to technological revolutions, and confront existential threats such as climate change and cyber warfare. The lessons of the Trump era serve as a stark reminder that international power is not static—it is constantly reshaped by political decisions, economic policies, and global crises. Whether the U.S. can reclaim its standing as a stabilizing force in world affairs remains to be seen, but one thing is certain: the wars of the future will not just be fought on the battlefield, but in trade agreements, digital networks, and the very structure of the international system itself.

www.ingramcontent.com/pod-product-compliance
Lightning Source LLC
LaVergne TN
LVHW061551070526
838199LV00077B/6999